The Lost Art of

WALKING
ON WATER

D0826724

The Lost Art of
WALKING ON WATER

Reimagining the Priesthood

Michael Heher

Paulist Press
New York/Mahwah, N.J.

Scripture extracts are taken from the New Revised Standard Version, Copyright © 1989, by the Division of Christian Education of the National Council of the Churches of Christ in the United States of America and reprinted by permission of the publisher.

Grateful acknowledgment is made to the following for permission to reprint excerpts, often modified, from previously published work:

"Future of Pastors: Woe or Wonder?" by Michael Heher, Copyright 1993, *Church* magazine, Summer issue; published by the National Pastoral Life Center, 18 Bleecker St., NY, NY 10012, www.nplc.org; used with permission.

"*Metido en la Masa,* Caught in the Mix: Reflections on Our Priestly Ministry in and among Peoples of Various Cultures." R.E.C.O.P.S., 1999

"Why We Still Need Theologians." *The Convergence of Theology: A Festschrift Honoring Gerald O'Collins, S.J.* Edited by Daniel Kendall and Stephen T. Davis. Paulist Press, 2001

"Words to Match." *Image,* summer 1999

Excerpts from "Why I Won't 'Cope,'" by Michael Heher, originally published in *America,* August 13–August 20, 2001 and is reprinted with permission of America Press, © 2001. All rights reserved.

Cover and book design by Sharyn Banks

Imprimatur
Most Rev. Tod D. Brown
Bishop of Orange
October 21, 2003

The Imprimatur is an official declaration that a book or pamphlet is free of doctrinal or moral error. No implication is contained therein that those who have granted the Imprimatur agree with the contents, opinions or statements expressed.

Library of Congress Cataloging-in-Publication Data

Heher, Michael.
    The lost art of walking on water : reimagining the priesthood / Michael Heher.
        p. cm
    Includes bibliographical references.
    ISBN 0-8091-4270-8 (alk. paper)
    1. Catholic Church—Clergy. 2. Priesthood. 3. Catholic Church—Clergy—Religious life. I. Title.
BX1912.H378 2004
253'.088'282—dc22

                                                        2004003010

Published by Paulist Press
997 Macarthur Boulevard
Mahwah, New Jersey 07430

www.paulistpress.com

Printed and bound in the United States of America

TABLE OF CONTENTS

Introduction 1

Naked 17

A Life, Not an Example 31

Never, Not Ever 52

Loyalty 71

Acedia 88

The Truth That Will Set You Free 112

The Near Enemies 135

What Old Dogs Learn 151

Select Bibliography 176

*"Everyone who moves on walks
like Jesus, on the sea."*

*All things die and all things live forever;
but our task is to die,
to die making roads,
roads over the sea.*

ANTONIO MACHADO

ACKNOWLEDGMENTS

None of these essays would have been possible without the support of my brother priests. To the presbyterate of Orange I dedicate this work. Particular thanks go to my *intimos* who spent not a few late nights discovering and debating many of the ideas you see here, above all Jim Forsen and Christopher Smith. From their candor I found my own voice. I also wish to thank Gordon Moreland for convincing me that I had something useful to say to priests, and to Gerald O'Collins and Norman McFarland for giving me the courage to speak up. To the extent I have learned the craft of writing, I owe it to Greg Wolfe, Philip Lopate, and the unrelenting support and guidance of Mary Rakow and Samantha Dunn.

—⟋⟍—

The aim of the priesthood is
to give wings to the soul.

ST. GREGORY NAZIANZEN

—⟋⟍—

INTRODUCTION

When I was in the college seminary, the rector finished my yearly evaluation by asking why I thought I would be happy as a parish priest. "The parish priest is the grunt in the trenches," he explained. "You end up doing the same things over and over: marriages, funerals, Masses, preaching. Parish ministry is filled with drudgery." He went on to compliment me on my creativity and energy and intellectual curiosity, as I recall it, implying that these assets would have very little outlet in the dull life of a parish priest. In those years, I felt the seminary administration would have been happy to see the back of me, but this was a new and novel argument: *Mike, you're simply too good for the priesthood!* I don't remember exactly how I answered him. What was I supposed to say? "You've got me all wrong; I am *too* dull enough to be a parish priest"? I suppose I jabbered something about feeling a call to this kind of life, which, of course, I did and do. But the stereotype he and others had of priestly life and pastoral ministry has, in many subtle and not so subtle ways, distorted how we saw ourselves and our mission. We priests have gotten used to not thinking much of who we are or what we do. When speakers come to town and tell stupid priest stories, we often find ourselves joining in the embarrassed laughter. Most disturbingly, we don't aspire, as we might, to be as excellent or as talented or as creative as we can.

We do not even expect appreciation from one another. To gain respect from the clergy, you need to do something different: get an advanced degree, write a book, give workshops, or work your way up the ecclesiastical ladder; in other words, you need to make a name for yourself for what you accomplish not at home but in those ministries and projects you perform outside the parish. There's nothing inherently wrong with priests doing any of these things; after all, I am taking time away from pastoral responsibilities to write these essays. But why don't we recognize more the very worthy daily love and care we give to our parishioners? How many other people can regularly influence thousands of people by their words? How many others know as much as we do about the inner workings of the various ethnic communities and social classes that fill our pews and live in our neighborhoods? Those in the know appreciate how each parish and school is a sophisticated operation that we run, with their help, effectively and on a nonprofit basis. Why don't *we*? We are even granted the occasional moment of absolute inspiration when lives are transformed by our touch, our counsel, our decisive priestly presence. In the care of souls, what we accomplish is often splendid and graced. This we hardly notice or allow ourselves to notice.

These essays try to show how our ministry is crucial to the life of the everyday church, how to be a priest is, to quote Robert Barron, "as exciting as being a brain surgeon, and as difficult and inspiring." The English noun *essay* comes from the French verb, *essayer,* "to attempt." "To essay is to attempt, to test, to make a run at something without knowing whether you are going to succeed," explains Phillip Lopate. Instead of exhaustive research or clarifying definition, candor and anecdote are judged to possess the advantage in bringing pressing issues to light. It is "the reverse of that set of Chinese boxes that you keep opening, only to find a smaller one within. Here you start with the small…and suddenly find a slightly larger container, insinuated by the essay's successful articulation and the writer's self-knowledge." The personal essayist believes that something of the whole forest can be known through his own experience as one modestly beleaguered tree. By wrestling with my own odd life as one parish priest, I am trying to find our priesthood.

I am a man in the middle. I no longer have the enthusiasm of my earlier days, and the years have disabused me of most of my romantic illusions about life in the church and the priesthood. Like someone who has pulled off the speeding highway, I am squinting at the horizon to chart how we got where we are and in which direction we ought to proceed. If I dare, on these pages, to ask some direct and personal questions, it is because I address them as much to myself as to you. You will hear my convictions at times, the ways I hope we might move forward together, as well as what I think we should stop doing; but please do not think I have an agenda worked out. My essays tend to raise more questions than they answer. I write from the heart out of curiosity and not a little loneliness. Are my worries and hopes mine alone? Do others, despite the daunting exigencies, still love the priestly life as much as I do?

Because it is a deposit we hold in common, a thing we have received and a gift that we give in service, I address my words to all who share this ordained priesthood. I speak to you respectfully in the second person, hoping we can find together the fit of a first-person plural.

†

We are all aware that priests today are beset, squeezed between declining vocations and rising numbers of parishioners, and stretched by an ever-growing array of needed pastoral competencies and languages. My situation, as an example, is not nearly as bad as others, but it is bad enough. There is roughly the same number of active priests in Orange County as there were twenty-six years ago, a feat unmatched by most U.S. dioceses, but the population of our local church has increased to nearly fourfold. My own parish now verges on five thousand registered families, and all our additional parishioners expect marriages, baptisms, anointing, funerals, and the like.

As someone who comes to languages slowly and poorly, I force myself out to greet my parishioners at the church doors before and after the Spanish Mass. Reduced to the communication skills of a two year old, I make many mistakes, and my misunderstandings only increase my sense of isolation and helplessness. Recently I thought a man was asking me about an item in the parish bulletin, only to discover he was really listing for me the schedule of activities for an upcoming feast day. Celebrating Mass and "reading" my homily in Spanish—there is little chance right now of my speaking extemporaneously—is the most exhausting and frustrating thing I do, and I'm sure it is no less exhausting and frustrating for my hearers. Our retired bishop is fond of saying, "This is not the cruise I signed up for," and every time he does, the whole presbyterate laughs in recognition.

Though the circumstances differ in other places, the demands are hardly less taxing. Pity the poor pastor in Indiana whose parish doubled in size and became bilingual when the local turkey-processing plant started hiring its workers from a small village in

Mexico. An entire county in Kansas is now served by a single priest who must circuit-ride across many miles to reach four different missions every weekend. Instead of closing parishes in urban areas, priests have been asked to pastor two parishes simultaneously, neither of which generates sufficient funds to meet the pastoral needs of the people.

My friend Jim, whom I consider to be the hardest-working priest in the known universe, was, until recently, the pastor of a parish of gargantuan proportions, and he did his job with good cheer and more enthusiasm than I could ever muster, or will ever muster, even in heaven. He thoroughly loves the work of a parish priest. So when he started questioning what's happening among us, my ears perked up. According to him, all we priests seem to be doing of late is "loading the wagons." By that he means we keep saying more Masses and celebrating more sacraments; we rush to more hospital beds and family crises; we establish new programs while maintaining all the old ones; we meet as many reasonable needs as we possibly can. Our Palm Pilots are filled with appointments and addresses; our cell phones ring and we know how to respond in whatever pastoral language the speakers use. It's hard work and there's never a shortage of hay or wagons to load.

Yes, it is unquestionably true that there are fewer of us to serve the growing ranks of parishioners and their expectations. The first thing we usually hear from our parishioners is their gratitude that we found time for them in our "busy schedule." At our worst we act like castaways, men seemingly forced by circumstance to rush and improvise and juggle just to get through the day. Everybody knows we are busy, but I don't think this is what we want them to know about us, not really, not first of all. We want them to know that we love them, that we are there for them in the ups and downs of their daily lives.

This is why it is essential, at this most difficult moment, that we do not allow ourselves to do a poor job or to work ourselves into nervous exhaustion or to lock ourselves up inside the rectory, all with the excuse that the demands are dizzying and sometimes crushing. At daily Mass each morning a woman in my parish prays "for vocations, the homeless, and an end to abortion," pronouncing each as if she believed them equally hopeless causes. Though there are days when we feel that way, let us try not to see ourselves as victims. We priests are not hopeless, at least not yet. We have plenty of resources, human and graced. And we have all committed ourselves to live by faith, not by sight, though I suppose none of us ever reckoned that *this* much faith would actually be required of us.

What shall we priests become under the weight of the daily demands placed on us? That's Father Jim's question. In our growing parishes, the priests, particularly nonpastors (in the places where such still exist), are relegated more and more to those activities that only the ordained can perform. Generous and well-trained laity do the catechizing, organizing, and managing; the ordained do the preaching and the sacraments. Behind this is an admirable ecclesiology, rooted in Vatican II: that all of us are the church, not just the ordained or religious. But the reasoning is also practical; due to the shortage, the priests have more than enough to do with their unique duties and should not be expected to do what does not absolutely require their powers. When I finish my morning shower, I often feel—especially on weekends—like just tossing an alb over my nakedness, as that's the garment I'll be wearing most of the day. In short, priests are becoming specialists—or, at worst, sacramental machines.

There is much to be said for this trend, not the least of which is that it helps assure the sanity of priests. But is a specialized priesthood what serves the church best at this moment? Is this really why the church ordains priests? And more personally, is such a life worth my lifelong commitment? In other words, was the rector prescient about the numbing drudgery of priestly life in a parish?

I don't think so. For the sake of comparison, let me hearken back to an earlier era and a different sacrament. Remember those who used to focus almost exclusively on procreation as *the* purpose of marriage, reducing a wonderful union to the functionality of an essential but single element? Vatican II restored matrimony's needed balance, giving voice to that love which nourishes both the enkindling of new life and the intimate and mature sharing of community. The priesthood was not so lucky. Vatican II did devote a good deal of thought to the episcopate and the laity and even restored the permanent diaconate, but it was less defining of the character of the presbyterate. We are to help the bishops, deacons, and the laity, but *how?* About this, the documents are vague, or rather, they are inclusive in a way that leaves plenty of room for interpretation.

From some quarters recently, there has been a push to emphasize the clerical character of priestly life, to draw up a detailed list of those things that only clerics are empowered to do and to insist that only they get to do them. The worry is, I guess, that the priesthood of the laity is insinuating itself into the ordained priesthood. On the other side, particularly here in North America, the push by some is in the other direction: to discount or sometimes discredit the notion that there is anything unique or important about the character of the ordained priesthood. *WE are the church, Father.* Perhaps the most passionate feel that if "the institutional church" will not ordain women and the married (save for permanent deacons), let's make sure it's so modest a job that no one would want or need it anyway.

For most of us, however, the relationship is clear enough. We live it out without much rivalry; rather, we appreciate one another.

Out of love, ordained priests minister, promote, preside over, and share the spiritual life of all the baptized (we do not give up, of course, our own baptisms at ordination!). And the laity appreciate the pastoral love, guidance, and companionship they receive from their priests.

This relationship is personal, not merely functional. We have been entrusted with the care for souls, not simply with the task of supplying the baptized with the sacraments. That is why I am not yet ready to be relegated to the role of a "sacramental minister," to be a ritual bit player in flowing robes who gives to life the veneer of the spiritual, a rabbi reduced to certifying things as kosher. Surely we did not work all these years trying to renew our parishes with the spirit of Vatican II simply to be left behind in the sacristy with our vestments on. In very down-to-earth ways and in each very specific place, we are to be "bearers of mystery," to adopt Robert Barron's very apt phrase.

If all priests do is "load the wagons," we will be much appreciated, copiously thanked, perhaps even generously remunerated, but someone else will be deciding where those wagons go. If I am working that hard to load them, I have earned my say about where they are heading, a say that flows from my pastoral concern, from a vision of what is needed by these people I love at this time in their lives. The exertion of a presbyterate is needed for the same reasons we need it from our families and our whole church militant, to press into service a forgotten but needed term. In a society that worships the individual and values the economic above all else, we need to preserve or renew the taste for something greater, even holy: a common life with love at the center, God's redeeming love. Catholics still crave this communality, or they would if we could show them how saving it is. If our parishioners are to be united in this communal purpose, individual priests will not help them by continuing to load more wagons—at least we haven't so far—despite our long and generous effort.

†

If the lives of parish priests were not precarious enough, we now live in the aftermath of a scandal over priestly sexual misconduct that has directly affected the lives of priests and people in thousands of parishes in the United States and beyond. The shock of it has horrified us all, and rightly so. Many priests feel ashamed, stunned that the young and innocent were hurt on our watch, and mortified that we did not notice what was going on, or did and didn't do anything about it when we might have made a difference. We are embarrassed and confused too because some of these men are our friends. Sometimes we feel humiliated because we are asked to explain actions by some of our bishops and their subordinates, our brother priests, that are not easily defended.

A priest used to be able to take the trust of his parishioners for granted. Not anymore. To some we have become a group about whom parents should warn their children: *Don't talk to strangers and don't let priests touch you!* Though we are not the threat they fear, we are not perfect. Every disclosure in the newspaper returns each of us to compunction and worry over our own past indiscretions. If one priest's hidden acts from years ago can appear in the headlines, will the light of day shine on my own crimes and misdemeanors, my missteps and the errors of my own youth? They seem pretty typical to me, even humdrum; but in the klieg lights of media scrutiny, I know even these can be revealed to look and sound shocking.

In the end, I believe the loss of our priestly innocence in the eyes of our parishioners may not turn out to be such a bad thing. It was an illusion, after all, a "collective fiction," this notion that priests were such good-hearted innocents. The role flourished because it was how we and many of our parishioners wanted our lives to be seen and because we honestly thought that such an image fostered the one thing priests needed from their parishioners: trust. Going back at least as far as Bing Crosby and Barry Fitzgerald in *Going My Way,* everyone agreed that a parish priest was honorable and practical. Jesuits were expected to be smart; your pastor was expected to be competent in those concrete things that engendered faith and fostered discipleship.

Above all, a priest, especially a parish priest, needed to have the common touch. It was all right to be good at basketball or golf or even cooking just as long as he was not *too* good. You were to fit in, but without too much familiarity or facility with any of the ways of the world. If you were bookish or sophisticated, you knew to keep it to yourself; one who referred too often to literature or the arts lost points for trying to impress. If you made money in the stock market, you didn't let it show. Instinctively you did not stray too far from what other priests were doing. Though your obedience might be begrudging, you followed the orders you received from above. The acceptable way to distinguish oneself in those days was a modest eccentricity, being someone like the absentminded professor or Mr. Chips; it added to the mystique.

Accordingly, one was not looking for serious defects in a priest then, as we did not look for them in doctors or teachers or coaches. Considered no more than unfortunate anomalies, the faults of priests were not to be talked about, let alone taken seriously. This may explain why those hurt by priests still carry the burden with such vehement anger and wrenching feelings of betrayal. Sure, one priest did, on occasion, drink a little too much; another was a reckless driver; you'd run into the odd character who could be harsh or impatient in the confessional or a little loose with the uses to which he put the collection, but these faults could be forgiven to protect the church and the priesthood. At least that's what we told ourselves. Even when one of us screwed up really badly, the general consensus remained that such matters were best kept confidential, if not for the "honor of the corps," then at least for the sake of protecting the people's trust in "the priesthood" or, most abjectly in recent years, out of the fear of expensive lawsuits.

Like our parishioners, most of us have good hearts and do love those whom God has given us to love, but we are not innocent and never have been. We sin, we fail, we let our hearts get calloused, and we can be as petty, thin-skinned, and self-serving as anyone else. And now our parishioners are more likely to notice these things, even comment and complain about them. Though annoying, this change has certain liberating advantages over the long haul. This pious image of ourselves, while charming and useful in former times, will haunt the effectiveness of our ministry if, as it obviously has in the past, it remains or is seen to be a convenient way for us to evade taking responsibility for our actions.

Start listing the excuses you hear made for priests and you'll soon fill a page. *What Father did, that's not his fault. It was due to his lack of formation in the seminary, or to the terrible assignment he was given, or because the bishop failed to give him sufficient affirmation.* People and other priests will point out the added pressure that a particular priest was under, or the constant demands made upon his time and energies, or any number of modestly plausible excuses. Haven't we heard a priest's sexual acting out excused in this way? *You have to remember, Father Bob went to the seminary in the ninth grade; he never learned how to deal with his sexual urges.* But wait, take another look: before you is a mature man in a position with plenty of power, respect, freedom, and responsibility, someone with many years of education and experience, a person others constantly turn to for advice and direction. Are we really expected to believe that he could not help himself, that he was the victim of drives beyond his control?

Embarrassing but true, we are saintly and sinful at the same time, just like our parishioners. Though it is sometimes claimed, the grace of holy orders does not conquer irascible human nature. We grow up, or don't, the same way as anyone else, and now this secret is out.

†

Since every scandal is presumed to conceal a deeper, hidden narrative, one even more troubling that what is already known, the sexual misconduct by our confreres threatens to sink us all. If once people were willing to think of us as innocent, others now are possessed of an equally facile willingness to believe only what is sinister and horrifying. Even though most of the alleged incidents occurred decades ago and the relative number of priests involved is small, some in our society and among our parishioners now suspect that the individual sins of some are but the tip of an iceberg, their revealed misdeeds understood as evidence of our collective hidden weakness.

Because of this, one can wonder if the priesthood itself has been discredited. Without our mantle of respect and admiration, have we lost our right to speak out as any kind of moral compass? It is not necessary, let me add, that we believe ourselves guilty, which most of us are not, but only that *others* think of us in this way. To the extent all of this gains a foothold in our own imaginations, it will break our confidence. We will end up testy and defensive, trying to exonerate ourselves with ever louder shouting. Or we'll feel defeated, glad to survive, thinking it satisfactory if we can at least avoid causing further hurt or embarrassment. How will that be of any practical help to anyone?

In trying to counter this possibility, do not imagine we are overcoming our difficulties by the current rhetoric. We've heard certain lines and perhaps we have used them with our parishioners: we speak of how these circumstances will be "a purification" for all of us in the clergy. We remind people of what the newspapers don't seem to mention: that the vast majority of priests are doing exemplary work and that only a very small percentage of priests are pedophiles. We argue that the typical pedophile is more likely to be a married man than a sexually repressed priest. We highlight the importance of everyone "respecting the boundaries."

Among these, we hear those zealots who go further and say, *Well, maybe this will finally force the church to make the changes it should have made long ago: to celibacy, to the top-down, male-dominated leadership, to secrecy masking itself as confidentiality.* Or if your sails blow in the other direction, you say, *Well, maybe this will finally force the church to go back to the tried-and-true and no more of this "wink-and-nod" complicity with those who aren't keeping their promises of celibacy.* Allied with this last sentiment is my favorite cliché to come out of the present crisis; it is delivered with a somber voice and reassuring nod: *The church will come out of this leaner and cleaner.*

Coping by means of slogans and righteous indignation is particularly American, I suspect, a necessary first step perhaps, but a distancing one because it objectifies the crisis as an issue out *there,* something to look at and comment upon. From such a perspective, we are not able to move forward, despite our genuine, fierce, almost desperate desire to do so. To make real progress, we first will need time to let the whole situation sink in, to know the struggle as our own, to get beyond all the restless talk to an uncomfortable but thoughtful silence. Only then is it possible that a thorough, considered response may indeed well up from a trustworthy depth within us.

After the horrors of September 11, for example, you will remember how the airwaves and newspaper pages were filled with talking heads, all offering authoritative positions vis-à-vis Middle Eastern politics, terrorists, security, and Islamic fundamentalism. Who holds those confident opinions today? Over the ensuing months, the unfolding realities have forced us to see that what was so clear to us then is now simplistic, more a reflection of what we *wished* were true, or *feared* might be true, than an accurate accounting of the actual circumstances. The real world is not easily named or understood or changed, no matter how much we wish it were.

The underside of a crisis is pain. And pain is not so much explained; it is felt. A natural reaction to turmoil is to hunker down, to try as much as possible to distract ourselves, to escape the anger, worry, and frustration that spring up after the initial period of shock, especially when our circumstances seem so overwhelming and, for the most part, outside our direct control. Or we cry out in defiant objection, *I don't deserve this! This is not my fault!* As in times of grief, the healthy response is simply to experience the pain; instead of fighting or running away, we do best to let it crash over us like the big wave it is.

Nothing reveals this truth so well as the *Pietà*. There is hardly a time I have come into my church without finding someone praying before this image. Although preachers have latched on to the last seven words of Jesus, I find the greater eloquence in the silence of a mother holding the dead body of her son. And just as Simeon had prophesied, it is obvious that the thoughts of many hearts are revealed in the sword that pierced Mary's own. In these troubled times, we might do well to explain less, and to feel more, to hold our circumstances in our hands without immediately attaching explanations or opinions to them.

†

The life of the priest in the United States has changed in fundamental ways, and not just because of the scandals. The shock came upon us quickly and has already rooted itself deeply in our hearts. But changes of the magnitude we are undergoing do not show their effects all at once. It may be that the real consequences of recent events will not become evident until it is far too late for us to do anything useful to stem them. It is quite possible that we will have to suffer them, that's all. But even this can be done with a dignity and conscious acceptance that is the opposite of defeat or resignation.

Beset myself, I write out of affection for the life we priests lead and in fear that, without a greater faith in God and confidence in the calling we have received, we will not be equal to our present difficulties. I have no interest in securing a protected place for us to unburden ourselves and lick our wounds. Rather, I am convinced that we will need to become different people from the priests we were formed to be. Like Steven Covey, I believe that "one definition of insanity is to continue to do the same things and expect different results." Yes, like the proverb says, old dogs will need to learn new tricks. Further, the only way I believe we'll have the courage to change as much as we need to is that we do it together. We will have to be bold enough to resist what the church—or at least what a number of our leaders—expects of us. We will certainly have to go against a number of the assumptions and expectations of our parishioners, as much as we love them and want to please them. The church shouldn't get the priests it wants. At this critical moment let us become the priests it *needs*.

The priesthood in our day has problems, hard and thorny ones that we must address with strength and resolve. But the priesthood itself is not a problem. For me and for most of the priests I know, it is still a privilege, a rare and precious gift, the specific path we've been given toward salvation.

—∭—

And Christ still sends me roses.
We try to be formed and held and kept by him,
but instead he offers us freedom.
And now when I try to do his will,
his kindness floods me,
his great love overwhelms me,
and I hear him whisper, Surprise me.

RON HANSEN
Mariette in Ecstasy

—∭—

NAKED

Sometimes, as priests, what we do is explain, sometimes we comfort, often we teach, we organize, we guide, we recommend, we direct, we supervise. Sometimes, both alone and with others, we even question and doubt and worry. But more often than not, we pray. Like Jesus, we find ourselves standing with arms stretched out from earth to heaven in acts that implore God's merciful presence and action; we often anxiously await a revelation of God's will, as Jesus did in the garden and on the cross. Our priesthood may well be defined as our willingness to stand in the center of life's tensions, alone and with the people of God, in prayer.

When Jesus spoke of prayer, he didn't really give lessons—outside of the model for the Lord's Prayer—but the way he described his Father said a lot about how hard praying is. When he claims that the one "who asks, receives, the one who seeks, finds, and to the one who knocks, the door will be opened," Jesus is perhaps a little ingenuous. Although this may be true over time, Jesus advises elsewhere that the one who prays should be as tough as an old lady demanding justice from a corrupt judge. That's your only hope of getting your prayers answered. Think of the Father as somebody snug in his bed, someone with every reason not to get up, a man so comfy that you must pound on his door incessantly until, out of sheer frustration, he gets up and gives you what you need. You must be *that* persistent.

This situation is not an attempt to make us cynical, for we are not to expect only corruption and a deaf ear. Jesus says his Father will answer with an egg, not a scorpion; a fish, not a snake. The Father is not toying with us. He does give his Spirit to those who ask. But a lot of screaming and pounding seems to be required first. Apparently we are expected to endure God's silence and inaction with demands and frustrated insistence. We are to make a scene. Don't wait until the morning, until he has had his first cup of coffee and is in a better mood. No, go ahead and bug God right now. Don't waste your time being polite, and don't be surprised if more time and further cajoling are needed.

Ostensibly the One to whom we pray is not surprised that we often experience him as seemingly corrupt, uncaring, or hard of hearing; God is not worried about his reputation; he knows he seems far less interested in our concerns than we want him to be. No reason is offered; that's just the way the Father is. One of the most ancient metaphors for the spiritual life is combat, and Jesus seems to suggest that the devil might not be one's only adversary; the Father himself can seem like a foe who needs to be roused or won over or outfoxed or overcome.

This kind of prayer is not what quiets the anxiety or lowers the blood pressure; it rarely leads to bliss. To pray as Jesus describes demands both the courage of a warrior and the docility of a disciple. In the garden of Gethsemane, he prayed with heartfelt honesty for God to let the cup pass away without his having to drink it, but then added, "yet not what I want but what you want." On the cross itself, at the very moment he was fulfilling the Father's will, Jesus cried out, wondering why God had forsaken him. Perhaps this is why Jesus says the kingdom of heaven can only be taken by force.

I am not violent like that. Thus my prayer often and easily, even gratefully, turns into something else. Into distraction. Into meditation. Into licking my wounds after yesterday's battles. Into reflection on the day's upcoming events. Into drawing up a list of the things I have to get done. There's something in me that wants to domesticate prayer, to siphon out the awe and tense uncertainty and replace them with comfy things of my own ken and preference. I rarely pour out my heart in candor and wonder, or in doubt and fury, or in whatever else may honestly bubble up from the unseen depths. I prefer to be most anywhere but that tender wound of passion and vulnerability. Whether consciously or not, I look for whatever returns me to rest. I once thought that being a martyr would be the hardest thing that could be required of a disciple, but now I suspect, at least for me, it is to remain in this fragile spot where I am not totally in control or utterly out of control, where I am contingent, in between, where I know myself as creature, sinner, disciple. It's hard to be naked—at least it is now.

This wasn't always so. Adam and Eve weren't the least uncomfortable when they conversed with God in the cool of the evening. Although the text is not explicit about this, it seems reasonable to assume that God too was naked when they walked together; he had nothing to hide from them. At least until the end of antiquity, many disciples believed it was possible to be restored to the relationship that our first parents had in the garden of Eden. Through his saving death and resurrection, they understood the Son of Man to have restored access to both the divine and the natural worlds. After years of purifying ascetic effort and persistent prayer, these disciples trusted that God would grant to some, while still on earth, the peace and harmony that had been Adam and Eve's.

We judge ourselves by our ability to concentrate at times of prayer or by the strength of feelings that come to us during prayer. But we truly succeed in prayer when we are possessed by the same unself-consciousness that our first parents had who, without giving their nakedness a second thought, walked in the garden with God in the cool of the evening. We best gauge the genuineness of our love for God by how simple and honest we are able to be before God. In fact, our prayer pleases most when we aren't thinking about ourselves at all (and, finger to pulse, how we're doing), when we are simply naked with God without another thought.

How did Yahweh realize our first parents had disobeyed him and eaten of the tree? Yahweh noticed that they were unexpectedly ashamed of themselves. "Who told you that you were naked?" he thundered. The serpent had promised that the fruit from the tree would open their eyes, and it did. What did they see? What they immediately saw, and felt they needed to hide from God, was *themselves.* Having to face God is not what makes prayer so challenging; it is having to face ourselves in God's presence. "It is absurd to think that we can enter heaven," St. Teresa of Ávila once remarked, "without first entering our own souls—without getting to know ourselves." If you want to know why we do not reach the intimacy of walking with the Lord in the cool of the evening, it is our unwillingness to see ourselves as we are. A hermit in the *Apophthegmata* remarks, "I believe there is nothing so painful as prayer.…Prayer requires that we fight to our last breath."

†

My first pastor, Michael Duffy, a truly holy priest, often repeated a sentence in Latin that he had memorized from the Old Testament; I don't remember the whole sentence, and I have tried—in vain—to find it in the Vulgate, but I do recall the last word. The gist of the Latin was that the high priest was required to enter the Holy of Holies "nudus," which he always pronounced with a twinkle in his eyes. Michael was a man of the old school when it came to matters of the flesh; he was so prudish that when we were watching television and he'd see a kiss—not a long kiss and certainly not the kind of passionate kisses (and more) we now are able to view on certain premium cable stations, just a simple kiss—he literally averted his eyes, often popping out of his La-Z-Boy with the announcement that he was calling it a day. No, that odd phrase stuck in Duffy's mind for reasons other than concupiscence.

It comes from the regulations regarding ritual purity that the high priests were required to follow before they went into the presence of the Holy One, requirements so serious that infractions could incur guilt and even lead to death. If a priest was to enter the sanctuary, he was required to strip off all his ordinary clothes, to bathe, and then, and only then, the naked priest was allowed to enter the holy place and put on the special linen drawers and other splendid vestments that were required to minister in the sanctuary. Michael enjoyed the image of the naked Aaron, dripping from the washing tub, dashing into the sacred tent to slip on his vestments; he sensed that the Holy One prefers us to be our naked selves when we come before him, not literally naked—such a thought would never have crossed Michael's mind—but spiritually or, perhaps better, personally naked. Might this too be an image for prayer, one specific to priests?

We are aware of how much we have to *put on* to be priests: the mythic image, the weight of representing the church, the outrageous demand that we act *in persona Christi*. But perhaps we have lost the sense of how much we have to *take off* as priests. No one talks much about asceticism nowadays, but it is essential to anyone trying to live a spiritual life, for it is the hard, human work of getting free of all unnecessary claims, especially of getting past our various illusionary images of ourselves, our fig leaves, if you will.

We all have projections of ourselves that block us from seeing that unique wonder God created and loves. But to strip off all those things is not so easy. A narcissist looks in the mirror and sees what he wants to see, or, at least, what he wants others to see; a masochist sees just what he fears. Only a saint looks in the mirror and sees what God has wrought. The Orthodox theologian and spiritual writer Paul Evdokimov explains it this way: "After Jung, psychologists know well that a little freedom causes anxiety but much freedom heals it. This is exactly the aim of asceticism: to transcend every limit, to expand souls by the audacity of love, and to develop the person by means of gifts and charisms."

†

At the heart of the rite of our priestly ordinations was the laying on of hands. Up there, very near it, was the anointing of our palms with sacred chrism, the other rituals being peripheral. What was ordained was *you*. Dressed in the best liturgical fashion or standing naked in the shower, we are always and exactly 100 percent priest. Our bodies, our minds, our hearts, our experience—these are the gifts Christ gives to the church. That guy in the mirror who obviously could use a couple more hours of sleep (not to mention shedding a few pounds)—*that's* who is ordained.

Costume and rehearsal often help, as they support an actor in a performance. I enjoy my own flowing vestments. But clothes do *not* make the man; and preparation is no guarantee about how we'll do at the critical moment, the *kairos*. When the time comes, it is you, you alone, the naked you; either you are equal to the call or you are not. In a crisis, in preaching, at the bedside of the dying, in front of a congregation presiding at public prayer, in the whispered words of the confessional, amid the heartbreaking circumstances laid before us in counseling, either we have it or we don't. Either we incarnate the priesthood of Jesus Christ or we don't.

†

One has to be the right *kind* of naked, of course. Noah shed his robes in a drunken stupor and Saul stripped during a prophetic trance. In both cases, the Lord looked dimly on their behaviors because they were not innocent, as the actions of our first parents had been in the garden. They were compulsive. They bared their bodies precisely in order to hide from their souls; the booze and the trance were ways to lose, not find, themselves. And this is not what God wanted.

Compare their actions with the behavior of David. While making merry before the Lord one day, David got a little carried away, something he was apparently good at. Though not unclothed, the cut of the apron he wore and the excited way he danced left little to the imaginations of the young women of Israel, a situation that delighted David as much as it offended Saul's daughter, Michal.

The Lord took David's side, and for no other reason than his winning spontaneity. He was just being—and baring—himself. From this we can infer, at least, that we are allowed to make prayer our own, even to make merry before the Lord if that's what we want to do. I think we can also infer that when, like Michal, we begrudge those who are making merry before the Lord, it is a likely sign for us to lighten up and be a little less self-righteous.

Actually, I don't think God really cares *how* we pray; if you ask me, he likes the company. I think God puts up with our distractions, our speechifying, and our eccentricities the same way the best of our friends do, and for the same reasons. "To pray," explains St. Thérèse, "means to treat God like a friend." Thus the only advice one needs about prayer is the Nike slogan: *Just do it!*

This is not to say there are not wrong ways to pray, ways that make it much more difficult than it needs to be to experience God's presence. There are even ways to pray that offend God. Jesus tells us his Father prefers the prayer of the humble publican to the grandeur of the Pharisee. Luke goes so far as to point out that the Pharisee wasn't really praying to God at all, since he describes him as praying "to himself." As, of all people, the art scholar Sister Wendy says: "Prayer is the only human action or state where cheating is impossible. As soon as pretense sets in, prayer stops."

Prayer is for those things that are beyond our means. God hasn't signed a contract to do my work for me. If I can feed the poor or comfort the grieving, I had better get to it. If, while bringing my gift to the altar, I remember someone is at odds with me, Jesus thinks I should first go and get myself reconciled with him before I make my sacrifice. You can't be both right with God and wrong with your brother. God is very likely to be unforgiving with the unforgiving, since the one thing that makes us unworthy to enter God's presence is a closed heart.

But outside of that, use whatever technique or style works for you. God lets each one of us find our own way. We learn from experience what works and what doesn't. And what works tends to change as we change; what brought everything to life in your youth will drive you to distraction in middle age; what worked in middle age will wither one day, and you will need to find a "new path to the waterfall," to borrow Raymond Carver's beautiful phrase. This is not a bad thing; in fact, it is a good thing. It does not reflect poorly on our level of virtue or dedication. Like any living, breathing relationship, prayer is allergic to inertia.

Clearly, David was a sinner, and probably a pretty lousy father—at least to Absalom—but he was a man of magnanimous great-heartedness. This may be one reason believers across the centuries have presumed him to be the Psalmist. The poetry of the Psalms has endured over the millennia as the voice of God's people at prayer because the Psalmist or Psalmists, David or otherwise, spoke as both one and the many. Our tendency today is to praise the individual, to applaud the one who defines himself or herself as separate from the many, but David and the other Psalmists would have seen themselves as persons whose lives incorporated the experience of the people to whom they belonged. They prayed in the most personal way, and in that prayer the whole people found words for their own experience.

Though later generations eschewed the term, Jesus most often referred to himself as a Son of Man, a Semitic expression that identifies humanity with a specific human being. It can mean simply someone whose experience is the typical or normal experience of "everyman." At the other end, the Book of Daniel uses the term to describe a transcendent agent of divine judgment and deliverance. It is possible that Jesus understood himself in both these ways. Here high and low Christologies meet, the incarnation and the resurrection. Jesus is the unique One and the Savior who identifies himself with the many, all of us.

Nowhere do we more fulfill this double role than when we are confessors. Frankly, I often go over to my confessional tired from other activities, hoping there will be few in the church seeking the sacrament. I would welcome a time to relax, read, or give further thought to what isn't working in my upcoming homily. But once I hear their voices, their words of candor and contrition, of frustration and worry, my reaction is a welcome identification. I hear why I am there, for I am no more aware of myself as sinner than when I am a confessor. A philosophy professor got me started on this path years ago when he asserted that "if there is a sin you cannot imagine yourself committing, you probably don't know yourself very well." I have my druthers, of course; certain sins are more attractive to me than others. But I am coming to see my sinful self more and more in each penitent. Precisely because I know their struggles as my own, whatever word comes to me—of forgiveness, encouragement, challenge, or question—is more likely to find a home in my penitents. Ironically, my sinner's words are more likely to tell them what Jesus may want them to hear.

Is it too much formal education, or perhaps is it the desire to see ourselves in a grand and admirable light? Why, as penitents and confessors, do we say what we think we ought to say, and voice not what we feel but what we wished we felt? Here's a penance for confessors: learn again how to be simply honest. The Psalms can help. In them we are returned to a directness in prayer and liturgy that is not the least bit careful or politically correct. You find in the

Psalms, without an ounce of squeamishness or embarrassment, for example, delight and vindication if the heads of the babies of their enemies are smashed open. "O daughter of Babylon, you devastator! Happy shall he be who requites you with what you have done to us!" says Psalm 137. "Happy shall he be who takes your little ones and dashes them against the rock!" The author of this malicious prayer may or may not have known better; we don't know. Perhaps he honestly believed that it was God's job to destroy Israel's enemies' offspring so as to obliterate the threat of their race completely, or perhaps the Psalmist sensed, as David would certainly have done, that he was letting his vengeful anger get the better of him, but he kept on anyway. Yes, such desires were ignoble, but in the rawness of that moment, that's what he felt and so that's how he prayed. Succeeding generations of believers—up until some recent pious liturgists—have not edited these sentiments out of the church's prayer book. If the church doesn't edit her prayers, why can't we just let ourselves go when we pray? Why in the world do we continue to pray as though we were trying to make a good impression on God? Haven't you noticed? He's already on to us!

Let's aspire to the same honesty as Job. Throughout his dreadful tribulations he was not afraid to contend with God. He would not curse God, but he would not be silent. He *would* have his say. He complained without shame and without holding back his passion. He cast himself prostrate upon the ground, saying, "Naked I came forth from my mother's womb, and naked shall I return." I was once naked, and so shall I end my days; in between, prayer will be the place I lay bare my life before you, O Lord. "Blessed be the name of the Lord."

A dose of this kind of naked honesty could go a long way to enliven our own weary rites. I don't think we intentionally try to deaden the liturgies we celebrate; we simply are too often not awake enough to notice how half-heartedly we pray, how we are giving the impression that we don't actually expect to be listened to or think that what we have to say might in any way be significant to the Almighty. There are times when the members of our congregations must wonder if we actually believe that someone is listening to our prayer and might even be willing to answer it with divine grace.

It is perhaps a sign of how far we have *not* come in the renewal of the liturgy that we priests do not experience presiding as an essential element in our own spiritual lives. We rarely expect to be moved by what we hear proclaimed at the ambo; if God wants to reveal something to us, we assume it will happen when we read the given passages in private while preparing our homilies. Too often we seem to be speaking more to the congregation than to God, as in those petitions we have all heard composed by those who use the General Intercessions to instruct us in right attitudes and causes. *That the people of God may open their hearts to the needs of the poor, particularly those being oppressed by the unjust social structures in our own country, we pray to the Lord.* I have even been at Masses when the presider addressed the words of the Eucharistic Prayer to the congregation, as though *they* were the ones being invoked. We think of the Eucharist as something we do for the congregation, which it is, of course, but, excuse me for putting it so bluntly, it will not work unless we actually *pray:* unless we stretch out our own arms and lift up our own hearts to be touched by the Lord.

Someone told me that in the Orthodox tradition, as the ministers leave the sacristy to begin the sacred liturgy, they say, "Now it is time for God to act." This is true not only of the congregation but also of the priest. When I expect something to happen to me when I preside, <u>I often find it</u>. This is not always opportune, mind you. It is embarrassing to have to begin your homily by saying, "When I read the gospel passage last week, I was sure it was saying one thing, but when I heard myself proclaiming it just now, I realized I had been wrong." At the wake of a longtime parishioner, a grieving priest might decide to forgo the usual poetry and speak with more emotional honesty: *Although we believe in the resurrection and eternal life, Lord, tonight we are very sad. We have lost Rose from our company and we miss her already.* At a penance service, a repentant presider might choose to be less pious: *Father, we are your sinful children, every one of us; that's why we are here. Sometimes our hearts can be so hard we don't even know it. That's why we've come here to pray. Please open the eyes of our consciences to see our sins accurately. Touch our lips to name them honestly. And, most needed, Lord, clear with your merciful forgiveness the debris that clogs our tired hearts.* On the few occasions that the Synoptics record Jesus at prayer in public, he did not strive for poetic effect but expressed most simply what he felt.

†

In my dreams, I occasionally find myself nude and lost, trying to get somewhere safe without being discovered. That's why I have a great deal of affection for the young man who appears momentarily in Mark's passion narrative. At Jesus' arrest in the garden of Gethsemane, the young man did not stand with his Savior, with whom presumably he has just shared supper, his belly still full of the Eucharist. He did not weep over his infidelity, as Peter would. When grabbed by the police and suddenly confronted by the likely cost of his discipleship, he was so frightened that he pulled his body out of his clothes and ran off naked, putting as much distance as he could between himself and his dangerous Lord. I wonder where he went. After he got away into the darkness, where did he hide? While Peter was warming himself in front of the fire, where was he on that cold night?

The church has traditionally presumed the young man to be the gospel writer himself, so perhaps we can also presume that the naked Mark came to his senses, returning to tunic wearing and to his Lord's embrace after the resurrection. We can do the same if we have run away from praying. Judas's self-knowledge led to suicide, but it can just as likely lead to reconciliation, to a coming to terms with ourselves as sinners who nevertheless have been called to stand at ease before God. To be able to pray in the way to which the priest is called, we have to strip off those fig leaves with which we have covered ourselves, some of which we didn't even know we had and only discovered in the moment of crisis. Aaron did it first. So did David. So did the Psalmist and Job. So presumably did Mark. If the rest of us follow their examples, we will find our true voices in God's presence.

That's what draws God near, the lure of the naked truth about ourselves. It's what God finds most attractive. To it he responds with passionate, spontaneous love. How do you open yourself to a fuller life with God? By seeking that original intimacy we had with God, by being as pure as Aaron, as spontaneous as David, as honest as the Psalmist, as courageous as Job, as relaxed as Adam and Eve in the cool of the evening, you won't care for a second who sees you naked.

—⟶ww⟵—

We need heralds of the Gospel who are experts in humanity
who have shared to the full the joys and sorrows of our day,
but who at the same time are contemplatives in love with God.

JOHN PAUL II
Address to Priests

—⟶ww⟵—

A LIFE,
NOT AN EXAMPLE

I want now to convince you of something that goes against almost everything you may have been taught. I would like you to stop being a good example. This is not to suggest that you would do better as a bad example; the bad example of our colleagues plunged the church into a crisis. No, I believe we would all be much better people—and terrific priests—if we would get out of the example business altogether.

I know I am probably a voice crying out in the wilderness here. The people of your parish expect you to be a role model for others, and so do your families and friends. You probably do too. Wanting to be admired is a very deep and automatic drive. When we stare in the mirror, our interest is not in how we look to ourselves; we look so as to imagine how those we meet might see us. We savor the adjectives by which people describe what they like in us. When we felt called to this priestly life, one of its natural attractions was the esteem that comes with it. If we work our tails off and shoulder the weight of our mythic standing, steeped in history and layered with tradition, why shouldn't we expect, in recompense, a little respect?

Such is almost impossible to avoid. Up front at worship, arrayed in colorful robes, all eyes are on you, your amplified words taken to possess a wisdom and power beyond those of others. You give invocations at religious conferences and Eagle Scout courts of honor. You pray at wakes and wedding anniversaries and picnics. At school boards and city council meetings, you demand to be heard. By the time you are done, you will have advised countless individuals and directed hundreds of groups. And if you're lucky, a goodly number of those who have seen you act and heard your words will have been stirred by your virtue. And this will please you, of course.

But it should be none of your business. Fulfilling a role, even a grand one, has monstrous drawbacks. And it is much less satisfying than it appears. Take a moment to consider the situations of three priests, each living admittedly admirable lives:

The first one is nice, a pushover in fact. Every time a parishioner dreams up some new idea, Father Nice lets him or her run with it. He also lets the staff do whatever they want; others even set his schedule for him. He is too easygoing to complain. He is equally accommodating with parish policies, perhaps even canon law, though we do not generally speak of this publicly. Private baptism? Sure. Don't show up to the classes and still want to be confirmed? Why not? Cover him with invective and abuse; he is too amiable to shout back. When a family doesn't get around to paying the tuition at the school, he's too polite to even ask them about it, let alone expect them to meet their obligation. That priest is the nicest guy you're ever going to meet; everybody says so.

But then greet Monsignor Pious. He's the one worth admiring. He is serene and humble. His clerical suit and vestments are never overly stylish or expensive. An indelicate word never crosses his lips. No one complains about how long he takes to celebrate Mass because one can tell, unlike with some other priests, how really holy he is. His genuflections fall and rise in a single graceful movement, and his bows are just low enough—not too low so as to draw attention to himself and not so modest as to seem unengaged or distracted. His eyes even flutter when he sings the Alleluia verse. His homilies are always well prepared, written out so he says everything just right, and delivered with a beautifully modulated voice, one sounding just as wise and calm and experienced as one expects of a saint, as self-possessed and grandfatherly as perhaps Walter Cronkite. When someone does register a complaint—about the misadministration of the parish or how the parking lot desperately needs repaving—he promises that he will, of course, pray about it. How can you argue with that?

But the one who surpasses Father Nice and Monsignor Pious is the priest known to be Pure. He's so humble, he doesn't expect people to call him "Father," nor does he complain if they do. He is liturgically correct and is fervently opposed to both abortion and the death penalty. He knows the scriptures and what the church teaches and can explain almost any text or canon. He is excellent in making his points when he speaks to the R.C.I.A. or the Bible Study. He is also fair in supervising the staff. The agenda and minutes are never late in preparation for the meetings he chairs. As far as anyone can tell, he has no noticeable faults.

No doubt, these are three admirable priests, but let me just ask you, and please answer honestly: would you like to live with any of these guys? I wouldn't. I wouldn't even want to go on vacation with any of them.

Can you imagine your life assigned with Father Nice? Since he says yes to everything, who do you think is going to end up saying no? And how will you look whenever you do say no, even on the smallest matter or for the most admirable reasons? Explain all you want about policies or the need for good order; the more you talk, the more people will come to know you as the one, you know, the other priest, the one who isn't so nice.

Life with Monsignor Pious is equally tiring. Have a couple scotches on your day off and look the worse for wear the next morning at Mass, and watch the old ladies' knowing scowls. If you were like Monsignor Pious, their eyes seem to say, you'd care more about the divine mysteries than boozing it up. Worst of all, you can cool your heels for weeks waiting for Monsignor to come down from the cloud of his meditative prayer to let you know what he has "discerned" about the project you want to start up with the youth group. And regardless of the answer, there can be no arguing with divinely inspired judgment. There's only one halo in the house and he's wearing it.

But the worst to live with, by far, is the priest who is pure. Because he always knows the *best* way, anything you do pales by comparison. Bust your butt organizing the Easter Vigil, and he'll point out how the "fullness of sign" was lacking in the way you meagerly poured the water over those you baptized. Don't vent your frustration about the staff in front of him; he'll only lecture you on how one best deals with the staff. He knows. He always knows. Do something good and he'll mention how it might have been better had you done it at a different time or in a slightly different way. But should you criticize him, you'll get back a four-page, single-spaced memo detailing how wrong you were, with quotations from scripture, canon law, and Mother Angelica or Cardinal Bernardin, depending on which side of the ecclesial fence he is on. He's the one who walks on water; that leaves you as the stick in the mud.

I admit, these priests *are* stereotypes, exaggerated to make my point, but if you have been around for a while, you know they aren't *that* exaggerated. We all know priests like them; perhaps we may have been or are a little like them ourselves. At least that's the reputation we have. Before the recent scandals, the complaints most often heard about the clergy were that we tended toward the self-satisfied. We seem to others at times just like the Pharisees.

The scribes and Pharisees appear in the gospels quite often, usually in debate with Jesus. The gospel writers use these confrontations to clarify Jesus' own theological positions vis-à-vis divorce, the resurrection of the dead, and the requirements of ritual purity, but that alone does not explain the sheer number of times they appear. I think the authors included the number of altercations they did because the disciples, especially the new Christian leaders, also needed to be warned forcefully against clutching on to the ingrained ways of seeing that the Pharisees typified, habits that may be defined as trying to fit new wine into the old wineskins. The problem with the Pharisees was not so much *what* they believed as *how* they lived. These were attitudes that the evangelists felt Jesus would condemn just as strongly among his disciples as among his Jewish opponents, as Raymond Brown has pointed out. The Pharisees fulfilled a role, a good one, but one that they used to distinguish themselves from others, not so much theologically as *morally*. They saw themselves as better than others. The Pharisee famously prays, "God, I thank you that I am not like other men."

Courtesy, piety, and competence aren't bad, mind you. They are skills, admirable forms of virtue. They work like the outrigger that stretches alongside a canoe to keep it from flipping over or sinking in rough seas. They set you into good habits at the start, such as regular times of prayer, being dependable, not letting yourself get too carried away with pet vices. Because life is swift and we travel through it without the benefit of much keel, we need these stabilizing balances, but they are hardly all we need. "The opposite of sin is not virtue," explains Paul Evdokimov, "but the faith of the saints." The outrigger should not be mistaken for the boat or for the ocean, a point St. Paul spent the whole letter to the Romans trying to make. It is a tool, not life. It's great for practice but no substitute for the real thing.

Let me confess my own pitiful life as a Pharisee. As I was rushing around before Mass one Sunday, doing God knows what, a couple came up to me and asked if they could help me. "Help?" I asked. They explained that they saw how "very busy" I was and thought they should come to my aid. Now if they had been other parishioners, those whom I liked more, I would have said, "Sure," and put them right to work. But I did not like this couple; they struck me as holier-than-thou and, worse, I sensed they thought the same thing about me. So I thanked them for their offer but declined. Now, as often happens after such encounters, I stewed about it, getting angrier with myself as I went along. Of all things, I did not want to be known as a *busy* priest. No, I wanted to be known as a happy priest, a good-natured priest, a guy who keeps a sense of humor about himself, the kind of fellow who might inspire others to go to the seminary because they could imagine themselves having a good time as priests. What bugged me was that I realized it was obvious I was not that happy priest. Why not? What was I trying to prove? Why in the world did I parade around as this serious, hard-working, very industrious priest whom I would rather not be?

Do you know what my answer to that question was? It was and is that I am good at it; competence is my best hand. I have a good brain, am well organized, and am not afraid to give orders. You want the ship to get somewhere, I'm your guy to organize the crew and chart the map, as those who have worked with me will likely tell you. But skills are powers that can be used for whatever purposes we want to put them. At that time, I was using mine to do two things:

1. Unconsciously I was trying to draw attention to myself, hoping to gain from the admiration of others what was lacking in my own self-image. Rush, rush; sweat, sweat; notice the hardworking, the dedicated priest. It was a way of asking, "See how hard and well I work? You are impressed, aren't you?" For one who was supposed to act humbly, it was a sneaky way to keep myself center stage, brilliant in the spotlight.

2. But I also used these skills to keep my distance, especially with folks I didn't particularly like. By my busyness I demanded respect or pity or at least notice, but not relationship. If pressed for a human response, I could reply, "Can't you see how busy I already am?" In fact, there's nothing better to keep people at bay than virtuous excellence. *"No, let me do it; I know how."* I didn't want their friendship and maybe not even their help, not really. I wanted them to see how worthy I was; I wanted them to look at me and, you know, light a candle or leave an offering. Admire me and then leave me alone.

This is how I would define a Pharisee: admirable, filled with virtues and abilities, smart, but not vulnerable and never far from the spotlight.

If you supply your own adjectives, you can see how easy it is to be a Pharisee. In those days, I would have prayed, "I thank you, Lord, that I am not like the rest of men: disorganized, unfocused, lazy, or like that priest in the neighboring parish who doesn't answer the phone for emergency calls. I answer all my calls, and if I ever do miss one for any reason, I always apologize."

Critical to Jesus is one's motivation. You are expected not only to do the right thing; you also have to do it with the right heart. I may carry out good deeds, even the very things that Jesus asked his disciples to do, but *why* am I doing them? Actual motivations are notoriously hard to gauge, especially one's own. I can tell myself that I do what I do for the love of God or out of care for the one to whom I am ministering, but is that really so? How can I be sure? Well, to answer that, I think the first thing to do is to ask myself where my real attention is focused. On the other or on myself? Look and see who, at the end of the day, is left in the spotlight. With a Pharisee, it's always himself; he must know himself as righteous. Another way to gauge whether your actions are motivated to support a virtuous view of yourself is to notice how disappointed you are when no one notices your obvious virtue. *Hey, I did something very nice for you; you could have at least said thanks.* So long as we don't truly focus unpossessively on the other, we end up sounding like that old line: "Well, enough about me. Let's talk about you. What do you think of me?"

If you ask your therapist about this, she'll tell you that it is called narcissism. *The Diagnostic and Statistical Manual* describes its essential features as "a pervasive pattern of grandiosity, a need for admiration," and, most significantly, a "lack of empathy." It says that narcissists

> routinely overestimate their abilities and inflate their accomplishments, often appearing boastful and pretentious. They may blithely assume that others attribute the same value to their efforts and may be surprised when the praise they expect and feel they deserve is not forthcoming. Often implicit in the inflated judgments of their own accomplishments is an underestimation…of the contributions of others.…They may ruminate on "long overdue" admiration and privilege and compare themselves favorably with famous or privileged people.

Jesus said pretty much the same thing when he noted how the Pharisees were keen for marks of respect in public and the best tables at banquets. In these self-promoting times, they would fit right in: Pharisees are the ones who want to be the celebrities, all fussed over and noticed. Flying economy class—steerage they call it—is beneath them; that's for the others, whoever they might be, those who are invisible because they are not in the spotlight.

The dark side of narcissism is the experience of psychic injury. I knew an archbishop who was exemplary in many ways, especially in preaching and his kindnesses to many of his infirm priests, but his exaggerated sense of injury was his fatal wound. No one thought of him as a happy priest though he was a very good, caring priest. When he was told that one of his priests had decided to leave the priesthood, he is said to have sighed, "Another ember on my holocaust of suffering!" This alleged comment expressed not worry about the fellow's decision but its effect on himself. If you kept on his good side, you were beloved and cherished; but cross him once or do something that led him to conclude you had been disloyal in any way, you were written off. Not a few of his unsuspecting priests found themselves cut off from his locus of concern, sometimes learning only years later how he had been offended. No discussion, no reconciliation, no forgiveness in later years.

Well, he's not the only one. Among us, I am sorry to say, there remain deep reservoirs of resentment and injury over past wounds or what we felt were intentional slights, especially going back to times when we felt we deserved a pat on the back, or someone should have stood up for us, or acknowledged our hard work, or otherwise realized how important or talented or loyal or long-suffering we had been, all those times we were not like the rest of men and should have been recognized for it! Legions are the ranks, to use an obvious example, of those of us who believe that they have been unfairly deprived of the rank of monsignor.

For long periods of time, we go along, enjoying ourselves, thinking these old wounds must have been healed or at least buried, but then someone pricks us exactly where we are tender and we're howling. Ask your friends if you want to know if it is true for you; they may be able to remind you of those topics, once brought up, that will lead to spontaneous combustion, or those individuals about whom you never have a good word to say because of what they did or did not do to you or for you. These are our wounds, and it is time for us to really address these injuries so they can be healed for good. The first step is the hardest, the most humbling: to see them not as grudges to be kept but as my own wounds in need of healing. "Wounds that are detected or declared," says Evdokimov, "do not grow worse." I can tell you this much: without such effort and much grace, you and I are very unlikely to ever be happy persons or priests.

This is one reason that being any kind of example is not worth the effort. Though we love the perks, being a narcissistic Pharisee is not very much fun—not for us, and certainly it is dreadfully tiresome for our parishioners, staff, and those we live with. In the gospels, the Pharisees don't tell one funny story. As far as possible, let us set aside the fact that we are people who are looked up to, or rather, let us try to get past it. Let's see it as the temptation it is and avoid it. Let's take the spotlight off us—and our supposed virtues—and put it back on Jesus and our parishioners, where it belongs.

✝

I think this is how we should do it; though it is a cliché, I honestly believe we do best to be ourselves. Let's try to be the ones about whom people say, "What you see is what you get." It is obviously far too late to try to go back to acting innocent and pious, certainly not now, after all the questions about our motives and the innuendoes about our character. The direction forward is toward greater openness and transparency. "He who wishes to be edified, let him be edified," explained Abba Theodore of Pherme, "he who wishes to be shocked, let him be shocked; as for me, I meet people as they find me." If we are to be rewarded, let it be, as it was for Nathanael, for our guilelessness. A humble, contrite spirit will not be spurned. Let's focus on the ways we *are* like the rest of men.

To illustrate my point, let me do a little midrash with the accounts of the apostles in the gospels. In contrast to the scribes and Pharisees, the apostles seemed utterly uninterested in reputation. You get to the point of wondering why they didn't demand that the evangelists make them look a little more uplifting. Think of it this way: what pope since Peter has allowed a story to circulate in which he is portrayed as a scaredy-cat, lacking faith and terrified of drowning?

If a Vatican monsignor leaked a story about the Holy Father rebuking anyone, let alone Jesus, might not that priest find himself suddenly reassigned to a nunciature in Antarctica?

And yet the gospel writers were not embarrassed to portray Peter as the fellow who always says the wrong thing. He blurts out what everybody is too polite to say: "We have left everything and followed you. What then shall we have?" When Jesus was transfigured in majesty, Peter talked of tent building. When Peter wanted Jesus to sign off on his own zero tolerance policy, he was told that he should forgive seventy-seven times. The gospel even reports the detail that he didn't dress very modestly when he was fishing. Please, is this really something we need to know about the first pope? Talk about offensive to pious ears!

At first, Peter refuses the request of his Lord and Master to let him wash his feet; then, in a reversal so dramatic as to certainly be reported in all the morning papers, he announces his support for total immersion. Although it is sure to cause scandal, the gospel writers were not afraid to report how, after getting a little carried away with the eating and drinking at the Jubilee banquet, Peter and the others fall asleep at the very moment when Jesus could use their support. Although he travels with Jesus, obviously hearing the Prince of Peace speak day in and day out of turning the other cheek and loving one's enemies, Peter still carries a sword and is not afraid to use it. Talk about bad timing: he asserts the unshakability of his faith on the very night he betrays Jesus. And he does so not once but three times, and not privately but in front of the reporters standing around outside the chancery office, waiting for a press conference to begin. And then, finally, there's that uncomfortable public dressing-down after breakfast on the beach. "Simon Peter, do you love me?" Three times Jesus repeats the embarrassing question. You can feel

Peter squirm. And yet, after Jesus, Peter is the most alive person in the gospels precisely because you see him for exactly what he is, including his faults and mistakes.

Though less obvious, the rest of the twelve are not portrayed any better. After having no more than a little trouble buying lunch one day, James and John are ready to call fire down from heaven upon the inhospitable Samaritans. Later they take Jesus aside, kissing up to him, hoping to score the best seats at the heavenly banquet. Of course the others are indignant when they find out, though the gospel is unclear whether their pique was due to the effrontery of the brothers or because the others had not thought first of asking Jesus themselves. The apostles are the ones who don't remember to bring provisions, the guys who so rarely grasp the point of the parables that they require remedial lessons. They are almost like straight men, feeding Jesus the lines he needs, "Master, why can't I follow you?" "Lord, we don't know where you are going, how can we know the way?" When Thomas is slow to believe that the other disciples have actually seen the risen Lord, Jesus appears the following Sunday and takes him at his unguarded words: *Okay, Thomas, come on over and put your hands in my hands and feet and side. "Do not be unbelieving, but believe."*

After the resurrection, you have to go to the letters of St. Paul to get this frank immediacy. When Paul tells you what happened at the council of Jerusalem, for example, he includes the sparks and details, the rambunctious debates and the emotions, at least *his* emotions. You come to the same conclusion that Peter did. Yes, Paul was in the right, but you also hear Paul's defensiveness, the obvious chip on his shoulder. (It's not surprising to read that none of his companions were able to put up with him for the entire length of one of his preaching tours.) Contrast this with the way the apostles are portrayed by Luke in the Acts of the Apostles. They have suddenly assumed a polished bearing nowhere in evidence in the gospels. If you want, you can say this is due to the descent of the Holy Spirit upon them—the grace of orders perhaps—but I suspect more human motives. In Acts, Peter preaches long sermons, rich in beautiful imagery and Old Testament referents, that is, homilies that were obviously ghostwritten by Luke, now himself a respected diocesan official. Times have changed and Luke wants his apostles to look, well, a little more apostlelike; in contrast to Paul's description, Luke's report of the council of Jerusalem sounds like something out of *L'Osservatore Romano*.

Here's one way to gauge whether you are an apostle or a Pharisee. Think back. How have you preached about the incidents I have just been describing? Have you been quick to speak of "doubting" Thomas, the guy we ought *not* to be like? Have you said, "Shame on Peter, who did not have enough faith, who could not stay awake or witness to Jesus when he should have! Thank God *we* are not like the apostles. *We* understand the parables, *we* keep the faith, *we* know better than to call down fire from heaven or to lobby for special favors"? And how about the incidents you draw from your own life? Which ones do you include in your homilies? How often are the stories about how *you* messed up? Are they more likely to be about how *you* came to an insight or how, by doing just what Jesus asks, *you* were able to save the day? No wonder the folks in the pews are checking their watches.

Years ago Chuck Gallagher, the father of the Marriage Encounter and other movements, described preaching this way: "You gotta start by saying, 'We lepers,' and not, 'You bums.'" Why can't the point of apostolic misdeeds be Jesus' wonderful mercy and generosity? *Don't worry if you don't understand the parable; neither do I. Thank God, Jesus is willing to tutor us. Thomas, yes, he had his doubts, but look how Jesus used even his doubt as an invitation to touch him.* Unlike a Pharisee, an apostle is likely to have experienced encounters such as Thomas's as moments not of shame but of tender intimacy.

I can imagine Peter writing back to John on Patmos, "In your last letter, you asked about whether to include in your gospel that unpleasant incident on the beach after the resurrection. You are kind not to want to embarrass me. But, John, please, don't leave it out. Yes, I was hot, I was really hurt. After all we'd been through, how could Jesus doubt my affection for him? But, remember, John, how badly I had messed up. I didn't want to have to admit it, of course; who does? But, hey, that's me too. I got scared and started swinging my sword at anything I could hit. And then I denied him, and he saw me do it. When he was nailed to the cross, I was nowhere to be seen. (Be sure you point out that you and the women did the right thing; you were standing there with Jesus as he died.) Yes, I absolutely want you to include the reprimand in Galilee; I want every reader of your gospel to know about it. I want them to believe that if I can be forgiven such terrible offenses, they can be forgiven too."

†

About a year ago, the police called me to the home of some of my parishioners. There had been an accident. A bunch of kids were riding on skates and skateboards, coming over a freeway overpass. The youngsters were talking excitedly, enjoying the speed they were picking up as the bridge bent back down to meet the earth. Unfortunately, a delivery truck was, at that moment, making a right-hand turn. When they finally noticed the truck, one of them was going too fast to stop in time. Caught under the back wheel of the truck, he died instantly. All of this was witnessed by his friends and, most painfully, his own younger brother. When I arrived at the home, the officer who met me at the door warned me that the situation inside was still, as she delicately put it, "unstable." I found the mother stretched out on the floor. One minute she'd be howling with grief, knowing that her son was dead; then she'd declare that he was not dead, could not be dead, how could he be dead? He had been so alive just this morning. The dead boy's brother was equally disturbed, asking me with ferocious agony why God had not taken him instead of his brother. "I am the bad one. I deserved to die. He always did everything right. He shouldn't have died. I should have been the one." Yes, the situation was unstable, to say the very least.

With us was a police chaplain, obviously a retired clergyman who had generously been willing to be called out on occasions such as this. But, God bless him, he was worse than useless. When the mother would shriek in pain, he would implore her to "have faith" in Jesus. When the brother shook with guilt and loss, the chaplain reminded him that his brother was "now in a better place." When he said that we should remember that everything is "grace upon grace," I had had enough. I looked at him and said, "Well, chaplain, I'm not saying what you say isn't true, but it sure as hell doesn't feel like it right now."

The chaplain was using the scriptures as a book of answers, comforting ones, he hoped, and yes, nothing he said was untrue or incapable of consolation. But they were all nouns, and nouns don't help that much, sitting alone, on their own, not in these situations. *Faith* enough to move mountains. *Love* all surpassing. *Grace* upon grace. What can you do with these nouns? Nothing but figure out whether you've got them or not. Either you have that faith or you don't. Either you have love that surpasses or you don't. And either way, there's no next step. Missing from the chaplain's obvious desire to help was a place, a context, in which his calming truths could find and touch their shocked and grieving hearts. He did not recognize what it might mean for them to believe such truths in these unbearably tragic circumstances, at the moment when all of life as they had known it was at stake.

In our preaching and in ministry, we need to keep in mind the ever-shifting context of our words, what at any moment our parishioners have "at stake." These are the verbs, if you will, that can help make sense of the nouns. I borrow the term from writing technique. In an essay or story, if nothing is clearly at stake, the writing will be lifeless because readers won't see why they should care, why the author went to all the trouble to try to communicate something. But when something is clearly at stake in the writing, readers keep reading to find out what the author has to say about an issue or an experience that the author has convinced them is compelling.

An example: I picked up the recent biography, *Joan of Arc,* by Mary Gordon to see what a thoughtful Catholic, knowing what we now know about psychological states, would conclude about the Maid of Orleans. Was she a mystic or a deranged mind? I started reading. Gordon explained the politics of the time, and that got me wondering if Joan was the warrior leader she thought herself to be or a poor girl being taken advantage of by the powerful for their own political ends. Was she the victim of manipulation or the one sane voice of her generation? All this was at stake as I read, as it also seemed to be for Gordon, as new questions arose and Joan became a more and more complex reality. What are we to make of her cross-dressing, for example? At the end of the book, Joan remained just as mysterious—no, even *more* mysterious—not because the questions raised were not answered but because she was more than the sum of our questions or even the answers Mary Gordon offered. Joan of Arc became more than three-dimensional; she became a revelation.

Almost every day priests are privileged to be present at pivotal moments in the lives of our parishioners. We baptize those who are born, bury those who die, anoint those in danger, marry those in love, absolve those who sin, and companion those who are troubled or lost. On most of these occasions, we are asked to say something. Here the chaplain and I are not so different; more often than not, especially in a tragic circumstance, I have no idea what to say. I rarely have a revelation. And in my anxiety, I want to skip to the last chapter; I want to confirm the ending, to assure them in this terrible moment that it all will work out. This I prefer to the messy and difficult task of working our way together through vicissitudes of the whole experience. Too often at times like this, I offer counsel, a noun or two that sum things up nicely. Advice is usually a poor substitute for revelation.

Again I think of Peter on Mount Tabor. The glory of the Lord is revealed to him, and his impulse is to build tents. Luke says he did not know what he was saying, having just been roused from sleep. But I understand his motive; he wants to be hospitable to their two surprise guests, of course, but I suspect he wants to hold on to this glorious experience. All of us know such longing during the last hours of a refreshing vacation or visit. We put off packing, we daydream, we pretend life could be like this forever, we linger in the comforting glow. Many of us, especially among the clergy, are tempted by what the Dominican Timothy Radcliffe calls "the sterile death of those who remain stuck on the mountain of the Transfiguration when the Lord has left." Because Jesus keeps moving, so must his disciples. In doing so, they suffer "the fertile death of those who have dared to take the road and travel with him to the mountain of Calvary…which leads to resurrection." Instead of nodding experts calling down nostalgic advice from the cloudy heights of Tabor, our people want companions on their journeys. Like Jesus, they expect us to accompany them in their howling and their stunned moments of unbending emptiness.

What is it that possesses us to make the gospel way of life sound easy? Although it goes against almost every word Jesus spoke, we aspire to inspire rather than to describe; whether meekly or forcefully, we sound too often as though we are trying to make a sale. Do we have so little faith of our own? Or do we worry that if our parishioners actually knew the cost, they would no longer follow Jesus? Why do we try so hard to make the gospel sound soft? Later, when it gets hard, as it always does, people feel betrayed and complain: *Didn't you tell me it was about coming to Mass every Sunday, about being a eucharistic minister, about sending my kids to Catholic school and using envelopes? Didn't you promise, I don't know, something about my yoke being easy and my burden light? In my recollection, that's the part of the gospel you seemed to talk about most. This taking up of my cross—all right, now that you mention it, I do recall that you did bring it up in passing one Sunday in Lent, but you didn't tell me so much was at stake. You didn't tell me what having cancer would be like. You didn't tell me what losing a daughter to drugs would be like. You didn't warn me how hard it would be to watch my husband of fifty years fade into the fog of Alzheimer's. Please keep reminding me that, in real life, something is always at stake. Shake me when I get all unfocused and sleepy, when I get sunk in the everydayness of my own life. Point out what I could lose if I don't change my ways or my attitudes. That's what I need. That will keep me going.*

Jesus said that you must take the plank out of your own eye if you want to remove the splinter from another's. We may not be so good at sensing what it is at stake in the lives of our parishioners because we too rarely touch it in our own lives. Thomas Nagel said something very obvious but that we often forget: "A person must live his own life; others are not in a position to live it for him, nor is he in a position to live theirs." Priests, even during the shortage, even during the present scandal, even we have a right to have a life. I am not talking about lungs filling and heart beating, or about bills being paid and tasks getting accomplished; I am talking about life lived at a depth in which each of us can name and feel and suffer what is at stake. Like everybody else, we give God glory by being as fully alive as possible, to steal a line from St. Irenaeus. Only by living a full life do any of us ever really discover what is at stake in it. So let's not use duty or responsibility or dedication or the danger of giving "scandal" or busyness as excuses to miss out on what life has to offer, or, worse, to hide from it.

Being so busy, we keep thinking that we need to get away to rest; we tell ourselves that we are exhausted and need some leisure. By this we often mean comfort and drift, time to play cards or window-shop or simply sleep the morning away. The French call this *divertissement,* and it is nothing more than couch potato life, as far from real living as watching golf on television is from playing the game yourself. We do not need distracting entertainments to help us forget life's difficulties; we need epiphanies, moments when we can see into life beyond the bright, hard surfaces. More than sleep, we need life. We need our vacations and days off to gain more experience, more depth as human beings.

So, go ahead, take that vacation week and go to the opera or the philharmonic every night if you come back more in touch with what's at stake. Go backpacking in the mountains for as long as you want, and don't feel the least bit guilty about it; just be sure you come back, like Jack Kerouac, more in touch with the pulse of life. Rent that villa in Provence or Tuscany, and let the life you find there come closer as you walk about. Stay up to all hours chatting if you want; it'll be worth it if, in the encounter, something precious is discovered among friends. Don't be sheepish about the couple of hours you spend reading each day; it is a time-honored way to keep in touch with what's vital. Out of what shall we minister if not out of this depth of experience?

If we find real life in our leisure, I think we'll have a much easier time finding it in the rest of our lives as well and in our ministry, especially in the lives of our parishioners. We will have developed the ear and the eye for it. And another thing will happen: if we "get a life," we'll stop trying to turn the ministerial moment into something to feed our own needs. We won't need to see ourselves in the spotlight. We won't insist on being right all the time. We won't waste time trying to prove ourselves. We might even become simple and forgiving, grateful and generous. Who knows? We might actually wake up one day to the revelation that we have been happy without knowing it, priests focusing our attention lovingly on those to whom we minister. We'll be apostles, no longer Pharisees.

*[The human person] attains its destined end through the body,
the soul's consort and ally.... In us it is not only the spirit which ought to
be sanctified, but also our behavior, manner of life and our body.*

St. Clement of Alexandria

NEVER, NOT EVER

One summer, when I was still in the college seminary, I got a job at a trash compactor factory. It was the hardest work I ever did and it put me in daily contact with people as different from me as I had ever known. My coworkers also noticed the difference, intrigued by my peculiar practice of not using the f-word. By contrast, these guys were almost poetic—no, *eloquent*—in the many baroque permutations to the f-word that they had at their disposal. Never in my life have I encountered it used as a gerund, an adjective, a verb, an expletive, and an adverb, all in a single sentence! It was as if the entire vocabulary of the English language had been reduced to a single root. My job, with the guy across from me on the assembly line, was to box the finished trash compactors and lift them onto pallets for delivery. He and I became fast friends because he used to smoke pot at lunch and therefore thought everything I said in the afternoon was hilarious.

When he wanted to know why I didn't cuss, I was vague: "I don't know. I just don't." My answer did not satisfy him, of course, and if anything, one has plenty of time on the assembly line. Back then there were apparently a lot of people with large amounts of trash waiting for compactors; we were working forty-eight hours a week. So, slowly but surely, he wheedled out of me that, yes, I was there only for the summer, as he suspected, and, right again, that was because I was in college. Then he wanted to know what I was studying in college.

"Philosophy."

That was a reply he had not expected, and he wanted to know, "Why in the world would somebody like you study philosophy?"

I had promised myself that I would never be ashamed of being a seminarian, but how would such a revelation affect the forty-eight hours a week we spent together? And what would the others think? There was no way, after lunch, under the influence, that this guy was not going to tell the whole crew. I took a breath and gave him the real answer, another certainly unexpected. "Because that's one of the things you have to study if you want to become a Catholic priest."

"A priest? No f—-ing way!"

Sure enough, by the end of lunch, the whole gang at our end of the line knew. The usual banter was replaced with questions; it felt like a press conference. On the other side, two spots up, a young guy who had just gotten married asked me, "If you're going to be a priest, doesn't that mean you'll, um, never, you know?" All of a sudden he became shy about sex.

"That's right."

More trash compactors float by, get boxed and loaded. The questions fade to bewildered stares. Then, picking up the conversation where he had left off, the newlywed asked again, "Never, not ever?"

"Yes, never, not ever," I answered. Now I was getting depressed. Never before had I thought of my vocation as something so remarkable, so dramatic, or so incomprehensible. These guys could understand why someone would go to college, although probably not to study philosophy, God help us; but to forsake sexual activity—that was an idea that had never occurred to them.

A thoughtful silence descended as we packed more trash compactors. After about an hour, the newlywed concluded, as if there had been no break in the conversation—and I swear I am quoting him verbatim—"Well, maybe if you never, not *ever-ed,* you could never not ever. But if you *ever-ed,* you could *never* not ever."

†

In former times, celibacy was related to cultic responsibility: only the pure could touch the holy. Whether you considered it a pedestal or a eunuch's gilded cage, it was accommodating to many of us priests because we felt not just set *apart* but also *above* the station of others, consideration granted us out of respect for our duties. No more. Many people, including a fair number in the pews, doubt celibacy's value. They believe it stifles God's gift of sexuality and limits the effectiveness of our pastoral ministry, since we are deprived of the appreciation of a pivotal experience in their lives. They no longer believe that celibacy makes us any more available than married colleagues in other denominations or the generous laity that also serve our parishes, a point I happen to agree with. Just as they did when I was coming up for ordination, many today declare that celibacy's days are numbered; the shortage of clergy will force the pope's hand. Some even believe that celibacy is what drives priests to anonymous sexual encounters, clandestine relationships, and shameful acts of depravity. And so here we are, in a time of such enormous ambiguity, defending our lives as we perhaps wonder ourselves why we're trying so hard to live a celibate life.

I do not regret my own promise; I renew it each year at the Chrism Mass. But I have to admit that when I hear myself referred to as a celibate nowadays, I feel like a mutant species on display, an intriguing specimen, a throwback to a more primitive era. In the general population and in the media, our celibacy is understood almost entirely as an absence; we are seen for what we are *not*. We stand accused of *not* being married, *not* having generative intimacy, and suspected of lacking sufficient loyalty to the conventions of family life. The celibate is someone to worry about, one who opposes, or at least fears, bodily enjoyment, sexual pleasure, and human comfort. Without knowing us, many conclude that we are lonely men. Their question is simple: Why the hell don't you allow yourself the full range of experiences available to human beings? Why live with a hole in the middle of your life?

There are a number of reasons people think of celibacy this way, chief among them an old-fashioned notion of celibacy, one coming back into vogue in certain conservative circles and with certain bishops and religious superiors who are taking advantage of "this present climate," to quote the phrase I hear them use. For them, the word *celibacy* is far too vague; they prefer the word *continence,* as in "perfect continence," a biological way of describing purity. They see themselves as part of a centuries-old tradition of sexual abstinence and purity. The goal is to be asexual, at least psychologically so. I call it repression myself, but it is a tempting solution for many because being sexual at least complicates one's life, and as we have learned recently, it can become dangerous, hurtful, even criminal. There's a reason the first things Adam and Eve chose to cover were their loins. Things go on in the nether regions and in the libido that are not entirely under one's control, as all of us discovered at puberty when erections would present themselves at the most inopportune moments. The sexual self feels at times like a Pandora's box that will certainly bring ruin if it is opened.

And now that some of our brothers, to satisfy their own urges, have committed terrible crimes, it is even more tempting to hope that continence or celibacy offers a safe harbor, a refuge away from the maelstrom of human desire.

Now if, by your promise, you are hoping to bury the sexual energy within you, I can't say that I blame you. In many ways life would certainly be less complicated if you could close yourself off from any relationship in which testosterone plays a role. But don't fool yourself; in doing so, you are making yourself a eunuch, and this is not at all the same as being one for the sake of God's kingdom. You are the guy seen in the parable burying for safety's sake the one talent he's been given. I am afraid you can expect exactly his punishment if you bury the gift of your sexuality.

Many of the faithful encourage us in this direction, however unconsciously. If you possess *only* what Edward Hoagland has described as "the beefy calm that often goes with Catholic celibacy," you will be much better suited to their expectations. Most of our parishioners think they want their priests to be those accommodating nice guys, the ones who are everyone's buddy, obliging friends who always have a moment to spare. We're the ones who are willing to put up with the clingy old ladies and soothe the volunteers when they are injured by touchy staff members or the crotchety remark of another priest. We are ever ready to lend our patient and confidential ear to whoever engages us in conversation, and yet, in our great courtesy, we never let the conversation wander to darker or deeper waters, to topics that might disturb the comfortable equilibrium. If anything, we priests have learned how to be polite. It is sweet of us to do this, really it is; everyone thinks of us as the nicest guys in the world. And I am not suggesting that we should suddenly become collective pains in the neck. But trust me on this: if anything is going to drive you off the deep end, it will be this.

A chameleon makes a lousy celibate. As nice guys, we get so practiced in our compliance that we stop feeling almost anything at all. Everybody else's feelings must be accorded our pastoral interest and respect; it's just our own that aren't. When we stop listening to our feelings long enough, we begin to stop feeling them. Our imaginative life shrinks. We become the men who have lost our affect. We certainly do not feel strongly enough about anyone or anything to speak up or disagree or fight or fall in love or weep. We can even get to where we know more automatically what we *ought* to feel than what we actually do feel in our hearts. Again, Hoagland's observation: "I tend to gaze quite closely at the faces of priests I meet to see if a lifetime of love has marked them noticeably, but too often…[I see] mere resignation or tenacity." When we live like this, do not think we are eunuchs for the sake of the kingdom; we are those who have been made so by others (cf. Matt 19:12).

If you want to know why we are not more prophetic in our preaching, it may well be that we have slowly lost the ability to even know what we feel, let alone to express and live by anything as strong and unyielding as convictions. Regardless of one's calling, a fully alive human being is a person who has strong opinions; he cries and complains, he cares passionately enough about certain people and certain causes that he will not be silenced or shamed into submission. The point is not to suppress desire, for the yearning for a holy life is itself a noble desire; what we discipline is our possessive craving, the insistent beat of "I want."

In order to figure out what we feel, we all need a place and people with whom we can be ourselves. If you don't have them already, I urge you to find and keep strong companions, people among the clergy, laity, and your family to whom you don't have to be nice and who will not mince their words with you, gentle but honest confidants with whom heart can speak to heart. I don't see how any of us can survive this era without sharing our lives with such friends. You can live a full life without having sex with someone, but I don't see how a life without good friends and intimacy would be anything but gnawingly depressing. We ought to worry as much about listlessness as we do about lust.

†

The book about celibacy that was in vogue when I was in the seminary was Donald Goergen's *Sexual Celibate*. As I read it then, it trumpeted the blessings of sublimation over repression, which was, for me, a welcome improvement. I discovered that although I felt more and more called to the priesthood, I simply did not have a talent for sexual repression despite my Irish upbringing. Instead of denying or pretending you didn't feel all those annoying sexual urges, at least sublimation allowed you to acknowledge their existence. You had something to talk about with your spiritual director or confessor. But they were still understood as a problem in need of a solution. You were supposed to exchange the passions for something else, to pour them into zeal for ministry or into the ardor of prayer or into the exertion of asceticism. The hope was that this transformation would dissipate the desire, that the air would be let out of the passions. And if this didn't work as well as Father Goergen promised, you could always fall back on the old tried-and-true: keeping "custody of the eyes," taking cold showers, and running laps until you were too tired at night to do anything but sleep. With repression and sublimation, the aim is the same: if I live rightly, these urges will stop bothering me. Both try to quench the thirst.

If it works for you, don't let me talk you out of such a life. But it does not work for me, and I'd like to offer you a different way of looking and dealing with our human sexuality, one that might make more sense—to me, at least.

Let's start by trying, despite all of our training and the "horrors of the scandal," to believe that human sexuality is, in truth, a gift from God, something precious to be cherished, not a problem that needs to be controlled, even for celibates. In the many workshops about sexuality that I have attended and will, no doubt nowadays, be required to continue to attend, I have heard such things proclaimed, but I doubt the speakers actually believed what they were saying. Their serious tone betrayed them, filled as it was with cautions about respecting the boundaries and the need to acknowledge one's sexuality, as though it were a depressing reality, like cancer, about which one was still in denial. Recently, besides attending to our own sexual integrity, we are to keep a heightened vigilance in our rectories about those with whom we live. All these things may be necessary, of course, but this is not how we talk about what we love. Is this the vocabulary that we use to describe what we cherish and take delight in? No, these are topics for abnormal psychology or proactive policing.

Sexual desire is not all or even primarily lustful, but you won't ever discover that until you let a little revealing light shine on your hungers. Yes, ever since that original sin, there is something disordered in our desires that requires vigilance and discipline. Yes, our desires, every single one of them, need to be purified. Our desires are like a magnet; though they do not aim us to "true north," they do get us near it, to something called "magnetic north." The disorienting pull toward self-interest remains. But to know ourselves, we must first accept, cherish, and thereby *deepen* the desires we have, and this is exactly what I don't think we do, at least not sufficiently. Most of us feel, when our sexual desire is awakened, that this is what we should *not* feel, that this is what we wish we *didn't* feel. Most of us don't yet trust that our desires, especially our sexual desires, are at least a "magnetic north"; that is, we don't really believe these desires get us close enough so we can recognize our real goal of love in the near distance. And thus, our immature sexuality remains for us chiefly a problem.

The irony is that once we learn to trust ourselves, we find it easier to adjust our conduct for the misdirection of selfishness. Yes, certain people who come into my office for appointments are more welcome than others because they are so attractive. Yes, in a bored moment, I notice who's cute in the communion line. I enjoy the curves that fill certain pairs of jeans and not others. When I feel the pull of attraction between myself and another, it is a pleasure, first of all, a normal, lovely pleasure. This is not called being horny; it is called being human.

Humans talk about what we love, and we hardly ever talk about ourselves as sexual beings, at least not in the positive sense. If you are so proud of your sexuality, who knows about it? Who knows the pleasures you take in being an incarnate human being? Who knows even whether you long for Ken or for Barbie? I'm not suggesting that we need to have a coming-out party at the Council of Priests or that an upcoming homily or talk to the Guadalupanas should detail one's sexual urges. But your best friend should know; so should your spiritual director, your confessor, the members of your support group, all those intimate companions whom you know to have your best interests at heart. What often happens is that we only talk about our sexuality when it is a problem—when we cross a boundary with someone or get caught surfing the net for more than the sports scores or when our bad habit of masturbation reaches alarming proportions.

In this, I think we have something to learn from this terrible present debacle. There is almost an epidemic of arrested sexual development among priests. Studies from as far back as the 1970s confirm this. (It is depressing to realize how things might have been different now had we done more to address it then.) Whether the objects of our affection are under- or overage, Ken or Barbie, too many of us have remained as compulsive as teenagers: outwardly cool and enjoying the feeling and appearance of being in control but inwardly preoccupied with lustful appetites. David Leavitt has described the closeted sexuality of Lord Acton as "a dilemma requiring the use of an ever more complex algebra of evasion." Well, Lord Acton isn't the only one! The proof of this arrested development is our *silence*. Our sexuality, like our ambition, is what we don't talk about. We don't talk about it because we haven't claimed it as our own or figured out how we feel about it, let alone be filled with gratitude for it. In too many ways we are not ready to talk about what we love about being a sexual person, even a "sexual celibate." About this we need to communicate honestly and courageously with each other, and I believe we, both as priests and as sexual beings, will not have gotten to where we need to go until we lighten up and have a sense of humor about ourselves and our predicament, when we are able to kid around about it. When we joke about it now, notice how nervous the laughter is.

I am convinced that a good priest has to be *as sexual a person as he can be*. Not less but more. I don't see how else to make it work. One way of looking at the priest as a bearer of mystery is that he is one who attends as plainly as possible to the pulse of life. Well, our sexuality is such a very deep and essential part of who we are, if we cut that out of the passion inside us, we stop being human. We become vanilla nice guys or the serene ones in the sanctuary with our hands folded, our embroidered vestments softening the lines of our bodies so we appear every bit the angels we'd prefer to be.

Oh, I don't mind having a body if I must, but I sure as hell don't want that body to dance. I try not to notice her perfume or to enjoy the pleasure of cheek upon cheek or the warming caress of breeze across bare flesh. Why go to the museum or take hikes into the wilderness? I don't waste time tasting the fresh pear or listening to music except while doing something else. I might be seduced by the beauty; I might know the wonder of being taken into the movement of bodies or even the sweaty pleasure and energetic camaraderie of men doing hard work together. I certainly do not want to feel that spark of attraction with another human being; it is the secret I cannot afford to know. Why? Because I might lose control.

Yes, that's certainly possible; evidence abounds to prove it; but such is not inevitable. This highly ironic situation is actually not uncommon in human experience, especially among those who have dedicated themselves to God. What you don't get to do is choose between your body and your call; both are gifts from God. Let us imagine for a moment that even celibates are made for love. To do this, we must imagine that sexual desire is an essential element in all human love, even the most selfless. Let us believe that our deepest desires are earthly and heavenly at the same time and that God's blessing can make them even more than that.

Now this is, of course, the opposite of what the church has often taught, or has been said to teach, about both sexuality and the spiritual life, with St. Paul and St. Augustine getting blamed for most of it. The supernatural is not the sexual. That's what pagan religions, with their temple prostitutes, believed. Jesus said, "At the resurrection people will neither marry nor be given in marriage; they will be like the angels in heaven." Yes, that's fine, but that's the way it will be in *heaven*. Here on earth we remain incarnate creatures, and despite the best efforts of the repressed, there are no asexual incarnate humans. Tell yourself what you want about this or that relationship, human love is never platonic. Just as we have had to let go of some older notions that do not make sense to us today—the church's support of slavery, the divine right of monarchs, the union of church and state—we should add the fear of our human flesh to the list. If you tell yourself that the body and its desires are too troublesome to be gifts from God, you may be surprised to discover that the person who would agree with you is Sigmund Freud. Much of modern psychology is based on Freud's view of sexual desire as animal urges that dissipate only through physical release. Ironically, this brings us to the far end from continence, focused as it is on a similar preoccupation with biology.

A friend introduced me to Sebastian Moore and his book *Jesus the Liberator of Desire*. Moore argues that desire is not relieved by biological release. (Think about it: if this were actually true, we'd all find masturbation a lot more satisfying than it is.) Rather, desire is liberated in Christ by a process through which I come "to want as ultimately as I am." "I have long been persuaded," Moore explains, "that desire is not an emptiness needing to be filled but a fullness needing to be in relation. Desire is love trying to happen."

I offer one of his sentences as a koan, worthy of long meditation: "Shame generates lust, not lust shame." At various times, I have interpreted the sentence in different ways. I have wanted to believe it is true, but I have spent years trying to see if it really is so.

What I would say today is this: if you're ashamed of yourself as a sexual person, your body's desires will be exactly what you don't want people to know about you, and a very deep and important place in your very identity will thereby always remain that lighted lamp hidden under the bushel basket (Matt 5:15). In an essential way, you will know yourself then as the one whom you hope no one will discover.

It is not surprising that, under the strain of your secrecy, you become the one who slips up every now and then, and then feels even worse about yourself, a shame that you also keep to yourself. You become the one who, while away on vacation, buys (never rents) that steamy videotape or DVD, who surfs the net and hopes the cops aren't monitoring the phone lines, the one who sneaks off in the afternoon to relieve a little built-up stress with a quick moment of personal sexual affirmation. In this, we are not different from many others: pornography, just in California, for example, is estimated to be an eight-*billion*-dollar-a-year industry.

But follow this path of lust and you will become that most pitiable specimen, a dirty old man, a voyeur watching life from a distance with unabated longing. This is loneliness masquerading as passion, and the price you pay for these desires is shame. Regardless of what you do or don't do, you will always *feel* yourself impure, and lonely besides, since you are not giving anything to anyone. The immaturity of the voyeur is, as Timothy Radcliffe says, his "flight from vulnerability." He takes no risks and shares no reciprocity. The voyeur seeks only "the safe refuge of fantasy that characterizes all unhealed sexuality."

I can tell you this much: if I had continued an asceticism of self-control, by now I surely would have committed some scandal or outrage. I'd have been one of the ones you read about in the newspapers. Sexuality's prodigious vitality is still both insistent and baffling to me, even as the years pass. Being chaste and sexual at the same time is a dilemma—and at certain times quite a dilemma—but sexuality itself is a gift from God that we disparage to our own loss. Its very insistence contains a thirst for something other than oneself. As one of my professors, Father Eluethere Winnance, said of Freud: "Don't tell me what I feel inside me is libido. I refuse to believe it. It is the desire for God. That's our deepest desire."

The great Mexican poet Octavio Paz says pretty much the same thing, based on his reading of the *Spiritual Canticles* of St. John of the Cross: "what the religious experience tells us—especially through the testimony of the mystics"—is that "sexuality transfigured by human imagination, does not disappear; it changes, is continually transformed, but never ceases to be what it was originally, a sexual impulse."

What living as a sexual creature means to me is this: I remain an open question, even to myself, one that is never really answered, and this leaves me unsure of myself, a person at the mercy of desire and longing, but—and this is why I won't give it up—in it I find and am able to give what means the most to others, my available incarnate self. Our goal should not be to quench this thirst; this is the *opposite* of what we should do. As celibate priests, we should be the ones with the bigger hearts, those known for their greater desires, for our depth of feeling, the bold ones who are able to be more honest and giving in all our relationships. With everyone we meet, we should enjoy sharing, with an utterly unpossessive sense of wonder, whatever glimpses and encounters we experience of the chill, the fervor, the terror, the bravery, or the anguish of real life.

My soul does possess immaculate purity, and I have not attained the discipline I hope to have over my desires, but these are not as pivotal as I had been led to believe—thank goodness. Like other forms of love, chastity is more about solidarity than control. In the poverty of a constant and gradual surrender of myself to God, by an acceptance of life as God gives it to me, in living as the poor must, from moment to moment, from grace to grace, this is where I find the value of my celibate life. This is what constitutes any spiritual life, of course; even were I married or living in some other type of loving relationship, the commitment would remain the same: to trust oneself to what is unseen, to accept never being quite settled in the here and now, to be contingent, at the mercy of a chosen other who, even when it is God, never gives you all that you want or need at any given moment. Besides, isn't it more than a little demeaning to God to make him a substitute for anything, even for human love? God is God. Period.

†

The only motive that can sustain real celibacy is the kingdom of God. Anything less just won't hold up. Knowing that Flannery O'Connor was unmarried and in precarious health, and likely to remain so, a friend asked her how she dealt with her sexual desires. In a number of letters, O'Connor took up the theme of purity but along lines very different from the continence advocates. "I do not think purity is mere innocence; I don't think babies and idiots possess it. I take it to be something that comes with experience or with Grace so that it can never be naïve. On the matter of purity we can never judge ourselves, much less anybody else. Anyone who thinks he is pure is surely not." Her friend pressed her for the reasons behind her chastity. "I have always thought that purity was the most mysterious of virtues," O'Connor explained, "but it occurs to me that it would never have entered human consciousness to conceive of purity if it were not to look forward to a resurrection of the body, which will be flesh and spirit united in peace, in the way they were in Christ. The resurrection of Christ seems the high point in the law of nature."

Just as a spouse draws the line against other intimacies to protect the union of marriage, the boundary of celibacy preserves in me a freedom for a particular kind of loving, a "no" that belongs to a larger "yes" in my life. I discipline my actions and chastise my compulsions not to escape or eliminate my desires but in an attempt to purify them of their grasping. I want to see more accurately, to feel more deeply, and to act out of a more radical freedom.

Everyone should resist turning another into an object for one's pleasure or advancement, but celibates pledge this with a specific dedication. In a world where people are more and more thought of as commodities, talent, and market share, our celibate love is a defiant countercultural act. With other objectors, we provide the needed protection of a refuge. Individuals are welcomed without an expectation of something in return; they can be who they are, even at times when they aren't sure who that is. I think people are so shocked by the revelation that some priests preyed upon children because the only thing they absolutely expected of a priest is that he is—or was supposed to be—*safe*. A priest does not take advantage; and his celibacy is the sign of that pledge.

What we give, or ought to be mature enough to give, is true human respect. Do not underestimate its quiet power. All love, celibate or otherwise, begins with an attraction to what one values. In sexual expression, it is the union of the self to another. In respect, the value remains with the other, a sight that is contemplated and cherished in situ. With long practice and much grace, the mechanism craving possession is broken or at least greatly weakened. Respect can then take on the characteristics of love; it moves from honor to admiration to suffering, which can grow into an enduring presence akin to prayer, a *caritas*.

Yes, to be loved is a great satisfaction but only when it comes to us as a gift. For that pleasure, we freely undertake a discipline that, once mastered, will deprive us of the considerable pleasures of being greedy and manipulative and patronizing and contemptuous. We try to keep something in us unspoiled, but not for ourselves. This we save for the ones we love; God first, parishioners, family, and friends next. We hope one day to offer it as a gift to strangers, aliens, and, at particularly graced moments, even to our enemies. For their pleasure, we want our smiles to be genuine, generous, and unforced, an expression of an honestly loving heart.

Naturally, a compassionate gaze will often go unrequited. They, not you, will look away. At the beginning, when this occurs, you may feel this as a slight, and the pain of being unloved, even unwelcome, will gnaw at you and keep you from doing what you could do. Later you see it differently. The pain you feel is not due to the lack of a desired response but remains regardless of the response. You keep your empty hand stretched out, and the love grows deeper, and so more painful, precisely because he or she or they do not reciprocate. I don't know why, but I find myself loving exactly what the other cannot love: I am drawn to what begets his or her fear or anger or numbness, my emptiness greeting another's emptiness.

Although I am still lousy at it, precisely when things heat up, I aspire to cool patience, and when the horizon turns boring and sterile, I try to persevere one day at a time. I long for a heart so pure that I will no longer suffer the tyranny of wanting the approval of others or the passing satisfactions of my own hollow assertiveness.

Yes, shock of shocks, priests can be as thirsty with desire as anyone, but we still try to love unpossessively. We don't do something; we stand there. In the moments when we experience a sexual charge and know that we are not the only one feeling it, we do not deny it, nor do we run away from it, nor do we piously pretend to be far too holy to feel such urges. What we do is suffer it. To use a misunderstood phrase in its absolutely exact meaning, we offer it up.

†

Of all the nonsense I have been subject to during this crisis, I think the worst was the suggestion, serious, I presume, by James Pinkerton writing in the *Los Angeles Times* that all celibates should be medically castrated so there would be no way we could possibly harm anyone. He presumed that the repression of our natural sexual instincts makes us deviants from whom people need to be protected.

Well, call me a deviant then. Celibacy makes deviants of us all, deviants from the prevailing avidity in our society for consumption and personal satisfaction. We follow a fashion, centuries old, shared by Buddhist monks and cloistered French nuns, defectors all. We turn our backs on the lifestyle that most people justly enjoy. We chose to live, however imperfectly, in the shadows of Augustine and Chrysostom, Aquinas and Hildegard, Francis and Clare, Ignatius and the Little Flower, Joan of Arc and the Curé of Ars. Whatever may be the current opinion, none of these struck their contemporaries as noticeably uptight or stymied. Rather, they invigorated the church and world by their words and actions, and their contemporaries were convinced that their chaste manner of life had a lot to do with it. By living now the way they did, even if it is presently less appreciated, chaste celibacy is a gift I still strive to give; and it remains, despite the odds, the paradoxical place where I receive what sustains my life.

By means of such a life and the grace that flows through it, many great ascetics and saints have aspired to walk about unashamed and unprotected, just as Adam and Eve did before the fall. As I mentioned earlier, from nearly the days of Jesus forward, some disciples were convinced that one could get back to the garden by human effort and divine mercy. To some of those who were not content to wait for heaven, God would grant the peaceful and loving human nature that once belonged to our first parents. The presence of such men and women were concrete signs that this sacred dimension had been restored to this world. Here is how the scholar Peter Brown described one such man, the great St. Anthony of the desert: "The greatest sign of Anthony's recovery of the state of Adam was not his taut body. In his very last years, the state was revealed ever more frequently in the quintessentially fourth-century gift of sociability. He came to radiate such magnetic charm and openness to all, that any stranger who came upon him, surrounded by crowds of disciples, visiting monks, and lay pilgrims, knew which one was the great Anthony. He was instantly recognizable as someone whose heart had achieved total transparency to others." To me, that is a worthy long-term goal for a celibate life, not to mention the best definition I know of a spiritual father.

LOYALTY

It has never come down to obedience for me, not in the strict sense. What my superiors have asked of me has not always been what I wanted; I have had reservations about some of my assignments and had times when I have felt completely unequal to the tasks handed to me. And yet I have done them and not just out of duty. If I wanted to and had a good reason, I am sure I could have declined. When the bishop first asked me to take this parish, I thought he was out of his mind. It was too big and complex, I told him, for someone who had never been a pastor before. He allowed me a day to think it over, saying, "There may be good reasons of which I am unaware why you shouldn't be the pastor there, but the fact that it's going to be hard isn't one of them."

I could have pressed him if I wanted to. Priests and bishops know how to count. The fewer priests there are, the more valuable each of us is to our bishops, especially if we are willing to work and are even modestly competent. Though we don't rub their noses in it, we have the edge. A wise bishop recognizes that he needs us a lot more than we need him; he knows he has to put up with his priests.

If bishops don't always have the priests they want, neither do priests always get the bishops we want. My naïve trust in the role of the Holy Spirit in episcopal appointments has been sorely tested over the years. I understand Flannery O'Connor's sentiment that when it comes to bishops, "usually I think the Church's motto is The Wrong Man for the Job." Yes, on occasion we have been blessed with inspired appointments, but judging from what any of us can tell from the outside, priests and people can rightly wonder how often that divine inspiration has been heard above the din of other agendas.

Moreover the present scandals have led many priests to doubt the respect they presumed their bishops had for them. A recent nationwide survey of priests, published in the *Los Angeles Times,* showed that nearly three-quarters of them were "very satisfied" with their lives as priests and yet had a great deal of mistrust in their bishops. Why did bishops delay in dealing with abusing priests? Their inaction or misdirected action has tainted the reputation of all priests. When the bishops proposed the original "Charter for the Protection of Children and Young People," only 34 percent of the surveyed priests gave it good marks. The Vatican and the priests noticed what the bishops had apparently missed: that if anyone was going to be hung out to dry in all this, it would likely be the unjustly accused priest. As one priest complained to me bitterly, "The bishops hold everyone responsible but themselves."

This is a particularly troubling development because it threatens the essential bond between the bishop and his presbyterate. Societies based on English common law are organized around sets of competing, if not to say antagonistic, interests. By contrast, ecclesial jurisprudence expects hierarchical collaboration for the common good. It is obviously a framework in which those with authority can more easily hide behind their cassocks, but I like its idealism. Who wants competitive relationships? Most bishops and priests—and deacons, too—prefer to see themselves as working in the same boat, ministering to and with the laity. Though we complain about them, priests don't want a confrontational relationship with our bishops if we can avoid it. Bishops have an important job to do, and most of the priests surveyed felt their bishops were reasonably good at managing their dioceses.

I think priests generally recognize how tough it is to be a bishop, particularly a diocesan bishop. They come in for lots of criticism—not all of it undeserved, mind you—and they find themselves frequently under both the gun and the microscope, with the same people wanting them to solve their problems and stop telling them what to do. As one who has worked closely with my own bishops, I have seen how the job exacts a heavy cost, which most bishops pay without complaining. Whereas in the past a priest showing any promise was presumed to secretly hope to become a bishop, such cases of "scarlet fever" are becoming more and more rare. When a priest I know was named bishop, he told me he received from the clergy as many offers of condolence as cheers of congratulation.

†

So then what does it mean today for priests to be obedient? This is hard to answer. I can more easily tell you what I don't believe about obedience. I don't obey because I am convinced that the bishop knows best. I do not place my hands in his hands because he possesses extraordinary or infused wisdom. Yes, the occasional bishop has the occasional great idea, but so does the occasional priest, deacon, religious, and layperson. There is a grace of episcopal orders, but intuitive intelligence is not what it is, as anyone who knows church history can see. Bishops like Augustine, Francis de Sales, and Oscar Romero appear only once every century or so.

Look back and you'll see that many if not most of the things that brought the church to greater life came "from below" and were often viewed with suspicion and mistrust by those "above" with the grace of orders. Eremitism and monasticism were born of the genius of outsiders. When the laity were not having the good news preached to them, it wasn't the bishops who noticed but St. Francis of Assisi and St. Dominic and their mendicant companions. St. Ignatius of Loyola thought he had protected the independence of his Society of Jesus by the additional vow of obedience to the pope, but even that didn't work; for a time the spiritual energy of the Jesuits was suppressed (from 1773 to 1814). Those in authority in the church have a long tradition of taking a good idea and trying to quash it, at least initially. Just ask Galileo. No good deed done for the sake of the church seems to go unpunished.

And yet I obey without anyone forcing me to. Why? For me it is the example of the theological architects of Vatican II. Today we honor their names, names such as Karl Rahner, Yves Congar, Pierre Teilhard de Chardin, and John Courtney Murray, but many of them suffered under a cloud of mistrust and suspicion in the years before the council. Some were silenced, often for the very ideas that would ultimately find their way into the documents the bishops and the Holy Father approved. When they were suppressed by church authorities, they remained obedient.

Their obedience was not blind. They were all too smart for that. They saw what was going on and were well connected enough to find out what was happening behind the scenes. With no guarantee that their inspirations would find acceptance by the magisterium or even by their local superiors, they put up with what was often unfair, wrongheaded, ignorant, even malicious. Confident of the validity of their own ideas, they chose not to take a confrontational stance in support of them. They believed in something beyond their individual opinions and beliefs, however impressive. They did not bolt.

Why did they choose the path of obedience? We don't know. Those under a *monitum* were not allowed to give press conferences; they are exactly those who do not tell their stories to reporters. They certainly saw few signs then that their setbacks would be short-lived. Teilhard died in exile before his ideas became widely known. How did they deal with the disappointment, frustration, and isolation their rejection represented? I'm sure it hurt. After all, these men loved the very church that was repressing them. No, there was no easy explanation for their obedience, at least none that I can see.

If I found myself in similar circumstances, I doubt I could go down without a fight. Formed according to the norms of Vatican II, including ideas by which these men enriched the church, I feel a responsibility to speak up when it is appropriate. I endure hours of committee meetings and write letters to my bishop in hopes of persuading the church to change the many things I think it should change. It is one way I have been trained to express my loyalty.

If I was convinced that a superior was going in the wrong direction or, worse, if I judged him as acting on an important matter out of less than the most uplifting intentions, it would sting to have to bend my will if it was demanded of me. When a priest is ordained, he promises his bishop not only obedience but respect. There's the rub. Respect must be earned. Without it, obedience would feel dishonest, as if I were surrendering my very integrity, along with my will and pride. I am glad it has never come down to a matter about which I felt strongly, for I can understand why some have found themselves unable to be obedient to leaders for whom they had lost respect.

The church is as human an institution as any other, as anyone reading the papers for the last couple of years knows. Having a divine mission is no protection against human manipulation, wrong-mindedness, or hubris, nor should it be used to excuse such behavior. Grace does not supersede nature; it builds on it. The problem is not that we are an institution but that we are too human, even for our own tastes. Since we cannot be anything but human, we must keep striving to be human only and precisely in the ways that Jesus was. St. Peter Chrysologus, Doctor of the Church, summed it up nicely: "Let us put on the complete image of our creator so as to be wholly like him, not in the glory that he alone possesses, but in innocence, simplicity, gentleness, patience, humility, mercy, harmony, those qualities in which he chose to become, and to be, one with us."

I believe the theologians who inspired Vatican II were right in their silence and their trust of the church; if it came to it, I know theirs is the example I should follow, for I can see the humility and patience of Jesus in them, as I see it lacking in those who mistreated them. But that doesn't really *explain* it; it only *describes* it. I suspect I admire their obedience precisely because it defies explanation. It is a mystery as deep as poverty and chastity, perhaps a far richer source of grace for me in our myopic times, where integrity itself is understood almost completely as an individual matter. They remind me that it is not to my own self *only* that I need to be true. There is such a thing as loyalty to the church, a loyalty that can at times require a disconcerted obedience.

†

Most of the time our loyalty is a downright boring affair. It manifests itself most strikingly in our surrender to the daily grind of shepherding the church with our bishops. The hardest form of obedience I face is the care and feeding of pastoral councils, school boards, liturgy teams, staff meetings, and the gatherings of the other parish ministries and organizations. Most of these can go for years without a millisecond of obvious transcendence; I'm glad enough if the meetings end when they are supposed to. So what? Did my mother feel anything but bored when she made peanut-butter-and-jelly sandwiches for me and my brother and sister, lunch after lunch, year after year? Of course not. Nor did she expect to. She was just being true to her vocation to care for us. This is a loyalty as selfless as that of the one who has been silenced or suppressed.

Our ministry is best when it can be a disappearing act. When we lead prayer or touch lives, we ought to be the first thing to be lost. Whatever may be exemplary or upright in our prayer or pastoral work is best known to our parishioners indirectly, if at all. Let them glimpse it in the flickering of the prayer itself, in the honest word whispered in the confessional, and in the soft touch of our skin against their cheeks during the sign of peace. We aim as much as possible to minister so that what they remember is not so much us as what God has done.

†

When I studied in Rome and lived with a hundred priests from all over the United States, I noticed a curious dichotomy among the men I knew. From some priests, usually from smaller dioceses, I would hear about the people they knew back home, their friends and parishioners, their bishop and brother priests. In the small talk after meals, I'd learn a little of their diocesan histories and what they had been doing before they were sent to study. Soon I'd hear of their pastoral problems and their diocesan accomplishments. Because I felt they were guys like me, I looked forward to the chance someday to go to their dioceses to see for myself what they were telling me. From other priests, often from the larger dioceses, I heard far fewer details of their pastoral efforts or personal anecdotes about life in their dioceses except tales of what Bishop So-And-So did to Father So-And-So or how the Fair-Haired Father Handsome maneuvered himself into this position or that. *Monsignor has been in the tribunal far too long; if he retires soon, as he promised, I'll move up to his post.* There was so much more talk about power and jockeying, not to mention gossip about who was in and who was out. These other dioceses I had not the least interest in visiting.

Is it too much to say that the latter attitudes were disloyal? We all had our ambitions in Rome; the Casa Santa Maria on Humility Street was full of prima donnas, including myself, all of us doing what we did with a view toward what could happen to us when we got home. But there was something sad about the way these guys saw themselves. They looked at the degrees they were completing as being their best shot out of—what? Ecclesiastical obscurity, I guess. From them I did not hear the vocabulary of relationship and belonging; they sounded like men who knew they were pawns and were determined to win the game anyway. There's the issue, it seems to me. Even though our self-interest and our vanity die an hour after we do, they are not to be allowed the center of our attention. We placed our hands in those of another as a sign that these concerns were now at the very least secondary. A loyal priest reins them in; he watches to make sure that they do not overly influence his decisions. He monitors them to see whether they are keeping him from being courageous or honest or generous in carrying out the tasks the church asks of him. He promised to take care of the church, not himself.

I think we need to help one another with this. In my diocese, we've got one another's number, no doubt about that. We know who wants what, or if we don't, all it will take is a couple of well-placed phone calls to find out. The question is not whether one is ambitious but whether one's ambitions are worthy. When any of us move back from the first-person plural to the first-person singular, we need someone to point this out to us.

†

A church that incarnates Christ is one that can be counted on, and for this reason I will be obedient to it. The poor will be fed and sinners welcomed, and not just when I or the other ministers feel like it or are up to it. Such a church creates institutions and procedures and laws and makes people serve on committees and boards to support the specificity of our mission. We stay where we are, or we go somewhere else, for the same reason. There's something beyond ourselves that takes precedence: Christ in the world.

I see him in our classrooms in faces flush with awakening and in the tired bodies of the confirmandi coming back from their retreat with their arms slung affectionately over each other's shoulders. I never tire of hearing him in the tearful promises of couples marrying. I am committed to an incarnate church so there can be a staff member available to help grieving families prepare the funerals of their loved ones and someone organizing the volunteers so that holy communion can always be brought to the elderly and sick who can no longer get to Sunday Mass. I like having a classroom we can lend out to the neighborhood Al-Anon group. I cherish the beautiful stained-glass windows in our church and the roses that stretch toward the sky in front of our church. I am pleased to find there is a place at the Chrism Mass for me each year—no matter what kind of year it was—to stand again and renew my priestly promises. I even appreciate the splendor of a sealed asphalt parking lot on which a parishioner will not trip on her way to adoration of the Blessed Sacrament in the early hours of the morning.

Yes, we ought to tread more lightly in this world than others. The direction we received was to be *in* the world and not *of* the world, a duty we have not always observed very carefully, with embarrassing results over the centuries. I understand the temptation. I am also too attracted to this world that God made so wonderful; I keep falling in love with it and thereby mistake the creation for the Creator. These are only our temporary digs, I have to keep telling myself. But would the Jesus who walked on this earth and on this water think it wrong to enjoy them while they are at my disposal? Would not the breakfast cook at the Sea of Galilee allow me to enjoy these gifts as long as I keep my focus on our mission, the coming kingdom of God?

†

In the heady days following the council, many of us often adopted a vocabulary of discontinuity, disparaging much of what had happened before the council as so many errors and mistakes. *We used to do this but now we know better.* To a certain extent this was as it should be; the church clearly needed reform. But as I look back, something else was going on. When we started speaking of the kingdom of God, we were going back to the vocabulary of Jesus in the gospel, of course, but I think the imagery was also attractive because it allowed us to distance ourselves from the taint of what we referred to as "the institutional church," a phrase we used as a put-down. Imagine the irony of this: for a whole generation you have loads of men and women, a majority of us with promises or vows of obedience, acting on behalf of the church and drawing our material sustenance from the church and yet wanting to consider ourselves as somehow separate from that "institutional church."

Since anything bad could be blamed on the institution, it was easy for us to get on board with this so-called Vatican II church. How could you complain about this theoretical blueprint and impressive set of guiding principles, especially when each of us was free to understand them in his or her own way? Our current spate of infighting, however unpleasant, may reflect a belated coming to terms with a church too much of the Spirit. Is it possible that young people's attraction to the conservative is simply a desire for a more incarnate church?

If you inhabit only the church of the Spirit, you'll feel no need for such a moderating virtue as obedience. Since you don't allow yourself to feel the attraction of feet rooted in one place or the pleasures of enjoying the passage of time there, you won't feel the comfort of it as your own. Your comforts are found elsewhere, in your theology and your practices. In an incarnate church, though, the day comes when you are asked to pull up stakes and move to another place or to do something completely different from what you had in mind. Then you feel the cut of obedience, even if your hand is not being forced. It dawns on you that whatever power or authority or opportunity you were given was only entrusted to you. It is not yours though it felt like it was. Upon reflection, you see it was never yours, not even at the beginning. It belongs to God, and you have been privileged to be the steward that tried to make a go of it here in this place and for the now that you were given.

†

One of the drawbacks of looking back for guidance to that first generation of disciples is that one finds very little attention to hierarchic order. Theirs is the world of itinerant preachers and small egalitarian communities, and so their questions were not the same as ours are. Much of this is attributable to their strong eschatological thrust. *What's the point of getting organized? We all know that Jesus is coming soon in his glory.* But Raymond Brown argues in his intriguing *Community of the Beloved Disciple* that by reading between the lines in the Johannine writings, particularly in the disputes found in the letters, one can deduce something more. The community to whom they were addressed was coming apart; one group and its leader were sure the Spirit was saying one thing, and another group with its leader believed the Spirit was asking something else. Without a mechanism for discernment among various spirits, Brown concludes, the community was doomed. What John's community lacked was an effective bishop, or at least a good pastor. If Brown is right, that could explain how, less than a generation later, you find something entirely different. Just a few years later, Ignatius of Antioch was telling his readers, "All of you, follow the bishop as Jesus Christ follows the Father." Why? Because they came to see that a community without the discernment of spirits would not survive.

The problem has a familiar ring. Often enough I am greeted by parishioners who want to win me over to the various inspirations they have received. Wild with excitement, they report what needs to be done here in the parish (often right now and by the pastor) or in the church as a whole. Though I try to duck it when I can, it is clearly and exactly part of my pastor's office to discern among spirits. Will this really help? What will be the reaction? Will it keep this community together? This is the downside of the "advisory" nature of various ecclesial boards: I can go out and find the very best advice there is, but the buck stops with me, at least some of the time.

The church leader—deacon, priest or bishop, abbot, provincial or religious superior—is no more likely to have the bright ideas than anyone else. God gives inspirations without reference to ecclesiastical office. But those leaders do have the job of discerning among spirits for the sake of the whole community, and it is not nearly as easy as it looks. One is not surprised to read in the Acts of the Apostles that when they had to do it for the first time, they decided it was easier to draw lots. The body of Christ incarnate in the church is a very complicated and rambunctious entity, as St. Paul knew firsthand; he had to keep sending letters back to the communities he founded, with strong advice and frank direction. Yes, Christ is the head of his own body but most often leaves those of us charged with its direction here and now to prayers of petition and our ordinary wits. Alas, none are infallible in this discernment but the Holy Father, and he is so only in clearly defined matters of faith and morals.

†

The primary act of obedience is listening: the Latin verb *obedire* is rooted in the ability to listen. To be obedient, the central question is, To whom will one listen? In the church's great multiplicity, there are many to hear. There is the Holy Father, and then there are the legions ever ready to tell you what the Holy Father is really saying or wanted to say. There are also one's own bishop and the norms, memos, mandates, and requests from his chancery that materialize daily in the parish e-mail box. I'm not sure any human institution has been responsible for as many experts as the church; if we go to all the effort to sustain these many institutions of higher learning, we'd be crazy not to listen to the experts they provide. Like so many gnats, there are also pundits of every variety quick to sort out for us every issue; occasionally they too have something worthy to say. Not least in worthiness is the *sensus fidelium,* that instinct in the faithful for revelation; as annoying as the most persistent of them are, many of the best ideas do come from our staffs and parishioners. Finally, in the silence at the end of an exhausting day or in the midst of the noisy debate at the Council of Priests, we ourselves sometimes come up with things worthy of salute.

I am ready and feel called to listen to all of them, but not in the same way. Ours is a practical task, and so I am listening first for what will work to solve our problems or evangelize our people or keep us out of trouble or whatever needs attending to at the moment. But our context is communal; we discern among spirits for the sake of the community, and given various ways to accomplish a given task, I'm listening for the one that will keep us together and enthusiastic about our work. And so I am loyal to the Holy Father and loyal to my bishop, not mindlessly or uncritically but fundamentally. I consider it a compliment of the highest order to be known as a churchman. My lot, and our lot, is with the church.

This means, I am sorry to say, that the diocesan bishop and the parish priest are men of divided loyalty. While I know I ought to be standing at the front pointing the way and leading the charge, I find myself more often at the back keeping an eye on stragglers, laboring to get the whole flock moving, more or less and no matter how slow, in the same general direction. A pastor is instinctively cautious like a parent, and not in a rush like the prophet. If part of me starts giving orders, the other part in me shouts back, "Wait a minute! We're not going anywhere until the supplies are loaded, the life jackets counted, and the crew has practiced the emergency procedures." When the discerner of spirits isn't looking, the pastor hands out towels to the elderly, asks the strong ones to hoist the youngsters onto their shoulders, and tells the timid that it's all right to lower oneself by degrees. He grants exceptions. He checks to be sure there is money in the bank.

Given the chance, I would choose the pastor's responsibilities over the discerner's, and so I am just as tempted as other church leaders to look with mistrust and suspicion on what may be needed innovation or courageous action, on the very prophetic ideas by which the Spirit might be trying to renew the church, especially as I get older and more set in my ways. But the point is this: we don't get to pick and choose, not really. We can certainly work to protect our flocks (and ourselves if we can); but the flock has to be going somewhere, and the discerner of spirits is the one who must call the flock to this forward movement. The Spirit is not given only for our comfort or our spiritual affirmation. Yes, Jesus promises us the benefits of an abundant life, but also sends the Spirit into the world to get us out there to carry our crosses and share the good news.

†

When I look back, I can't say that my average is particularly impressive. As a discerner of spirits, I am proud that certain things worked out, by which I mean, the winds of the Spirit seemed to fill those sails and carry us along toward something useful. But I have also, like Sisyphus with his rock, stubbornly pursued certain inspirations despite plenty of contrary evidence that should have given me pause. And of course, though I didn't see it at the time, that old devil, ego, fooled me over and over; when I got on my high horse, it was more often out of wounded pride than the defense of any holy principle; the Spirit had very little to do with it. This is why priests, especially pastors, are usually ready to cut their bishops a lot of slack, forgiving in them a similar lack of spiritual acumen.

†

I am loyal to the church because I see Christ incarnate in it. Sometimes it is the resurrected Christ I meet, but often enough it is the still wounded, still suffering Christ. I remain loyal not because church leaders, including myself, are right. Despite the long efforts of most disciples and the ever abundant grace of God, we remain a disordered church of sinners, ever in need of reform, the ordained no less than the laity. Each of us and all of us struggle against blindness, insensitivity, and hard-heartedness, that is, against sin and ignorance. If such things appall me in my bishop and in my parishioners, I am no less appalled by them in myself.

Despite all that, Christ is still alive; I see him every day, even in myself, and I am grateful to be counted a member of his body. Being with my parishioners, baptizing their babies, helping in their projects, instructing their children, cheering them on when they inspire others, burying their parents, sharing their lives and their burdens, here I see Christ at work. I also see Christ in the common effort I share with my bishop, my brother priests, the deacons, and other church leaders, up to our elbows in the messy work of discernment among spirits.

I take my lead from Christ. If anyone should have been put off by all our sinfulness and weakness, it should have been the sinless Christ. It was not because he found us particularly just or worthy that Jesus died for us; rather, "God shows his love for us in that while we were yet sinners Christ died for us" (Rom 5:6–8). If Christ humbled himself, even emptied himself, for the likes of us, I am obedient to sinners out of a much more modest but matching conviction and sacrifice. Though it may never be known to others, it is a way I proclaim that who I am, what I do, how I live, and whether I am a success or failure here on earth—all of this and everything else about me—are not really about me, not anymore; to the extent I can, it is now all about Christ, his life, his redemption. I abandon my fate to Christ in the church.

*And God converted the dryness of
my soul into a great tenderness.*

ST. TERESA OF ÁVILA

∿

ACEDIA

Have you run into this priest? He does the same things as you—not an overly taxing slate of events, just the normal things that all of us do without thinking—yet they appear to take a lot more out of him than they do out of you. He seems to have a case of perpetual jet lag, he is always sighing. When you ask him what's wrong, he replies, "Nothing. I'm just a little tired, I guess." He doesn't sound tired, though; he sounds sad.

But it can't be for the reasons he articulates. Oh, he has his complaints, all right. He worries about lots of things—all of them, to you, small potatoes. *So what if the housekeeper cooked the same thing twice in one month? Why get bent out of shape all of a sudden because the youth minister is flaky about turning in receipts?* He compares how *this* parish is not what the last one was or what the one to which he thinks he should be assigned will be, a place where he is convinced his skills won't be wasted on so many trivial affairs. *The people here, well, they aren't all that interesting; their concerns are so narrow.* He complains that it's impossible even to find a companionable parishioner for golf.

With the people he may be kind and observant of his responsibilities, but he gets no perceivable enjoyment from anointing the sick, hearing confessions, or celebrating Mass. Though he may celebrate these sacraments well enough, the parishioners hear the weary detachment in his voice, as if he is slightly annoyed to have to deal with them. He figures ways to cut back on his duties, hoping the change will assuage his restless fatigue. But how can this priest suffer burnout when he isn't even lit?

He confesses that he doesn't sleep well, has little appetite, or binges on late-night snacks. You wonder if he isn't tossing back a couple of shots with his snacks, but you don't say anything. After all, he gets up for Mass; he does most of what he is supposed to do.

You wait, trying to be patient, but he doesn't get any better. You encourage him to get together with his friends, something he has stopped doing, but he tells you how tired he is of their nonsense. *Every week, we do the same thing, complain about the same problems, and tell the same old stories. No, I've had it with them.* The only emotion that seems to rise out of the silent depths is a nagging anxiety, and this is what makes living with him most difficult. Chaucer's Parson described him as "a man...annoyed with his own life."

Have you ever met this priest? I have. I have even *been* that priest myself.

†

The malady he suffers from has been found across the ages in the literature of almost every society. It has gone by many names. Aristotle described it, so did Hippocrates, using the term *melancholia.* The desert monks called it *acedia,* which they considered one of the deadly sins. Later generations translated that word as sloth or faintheartedness or confusion or sorrow or dread or listlessness. We use a variety of terms for it today: we say someone is depressed, or burnt out, or having a midlife crisis. They can all be ways of describing the experience Dante captured so poignantly in the first canto of his *Comedy:*

> *When I had journeyed half of our life's way,*
> *I found myself within a shadowed forest,*
> *for I had lost the path that does not stray.*
> *Ah, it is hard to speak of what it was,*
> *that savage forest, dense and difficult,*
> *which even in recall renews my fear:*
> *So bitter—death is hardly more severe!*

I favor the monks' term, *acedia,* because, at least for me, the struggle has been primarily spiritual. In describing the dark night of the soul, St. John of the Cross compares this experience in prayer to that of a lover whose affections have been withdrawn without explanation. The sentiments and encouragement that have sustained me in prayer fade, and the sense of God's presence evaporates. No one is listening and nothing is coming to me from the other side. The solitude that used to heal me no longer does. I tire of the silence. Since prayer feels like a complete waste of time, I have often been tempted to abandon it altogether. Though I haven't quite done that, out of sheer boredom and frustration, I let myself fill the blankness by reading books of meditation and spiritual reading.

In an annoying haze, I browse the large section of shelves devoted to prayer in our local Catholic bookstore, seeking counsel from the saints and mystics. From them, I obtain the voyeur's pleasure of seeing those who are really in union with God. What is lacking in my own prayer is exactly what intrigues me on the pages: that

romantic grandeur or strong sensation of presence, the inspiration
of being caught up in something beyond oneself, or in an intimation
of authenticity, or delight or inspiration. Sometimes knowing that
someone once felt these noble sentiments confirms in me a modest
sense of hope, a confidence that if I soldier on, perhaps things will
become better. After all, the saints had their own struggles. But at
other times, the comparison between their mystic heights and the
muddle of my distracted emptiness is only demoralizing.

Of course, I suspect this situation must be my fault in some
way. I speculate that God would reward me again if I could rid
myself of these pesky sins and faults. Or perhaps I could hear God
better if I prayed in a different way. Or something could get through
to me if I could force myself to be less distracted and more disci-
plined. Perhaps *this*—whichever *this*—could jump-start my spiritual life; perhaps *this* could make me zealous again.

But it is not like that with acedia. One's earnest *fervorinos* and
firm purposes of amendment do not free one from its grip, not by a
long shot. It is much more complicated than that, and though it
does not feel that way, acedia is a significant occasion in one's spiritual life if my heroes, the desert fathers and mothers, are to be
trusted. When they spoke of acedia as a deadly sin, they did not
mean it as we think of sin, as a fault committed by an individual, as
a personal moral failure. They thought of a deadly sin more like
quicksand, as a force that attracted its victims away from the growth
and maturity and holiness they had committed themselves to find.
Giving into this temptation, that would be a person's sin, yes, but the
situation itself, as St. Cyril of Jerusalem described such passages,
was a dangerous but important turning point: "The dragon is at the
side of the road watching those who pass. Take care lest he devour

you! You are going to the Father of Souls, but it is necessary to pass by the dragon."

In our sunny post–Vatican II spirituality, we talk a lot about the gifts of the Spirit, about grace and about faith, but it is possible that we have forgotten the danger posed by the dragons. We believe, or at least we give the impression that we believe the spiritual life can be lived without much effort or risk and even that the spiritual life, properly lived, can act as a vaccine against the stresses of real life, a way around or above all that can be harsh and unforgiving. Even though God does do most of the work in our lives by his grace, living for God is the most dangerous thing we can do with our lives. It is the opposite of a "Get out of jail free" card. It complicates our lives and changes our direction and calls us past everything we thought we knew. Rather, the promise to protect one from the pain in one's life is the allure of the deadly sins.

The church named the particular dragon of acedia the "noonday demon," based on Jerome's translation of Psalm 91:6: *daemonio meridiano.* "The devastating plague at noon" was the thing that you could see clearly in the brightest part of the day, according to St. John Cassian, but that nonetheless comes to wretch your soul away from God. The other deadly sins require a certain darkness to thrive. If you are going to kill an enemy, for example, you close off your mind to any positive feelings toward your victim, feelings that might mitigate your resolve. For the sake of the present passion, lovers intent on adultery close their hearts, at least momentarily, to their spouses. But acedia shamelessly stares you right in the face. "Depression stands in the full glare of the sun, unchallenged by recognition," explains Andrew Solomon in his comprehensive, accurate, and very helpful chronicle of acedia, *The Noonday Demon.* "You can know all the why and the wherefore and suffer just as much as if you were shrouded in ignorance." The mystics called it a form of purification; good for them, but an elegant label offers little comfort. The real danger in depression is the fact that it is "a sadness proximate to truth," as Thomas Gray described it in his famous "Elegy Written in a Country Churchyard." It feels so real you believe it is the way things really are.

Unaddressed, acedia leads, among other things, to cynicism, a well-known occupational hazard of the clergy, as the following stories tell.

The first is an old tale told about the installation of a new monsignor. Like some among us, the poor cleric had been anxiously awaiting this papal honor for more years than he deserved, or so he, in all his humility, felt. And so when the good news finally arrived, he already knew exactly how he wanted the installation ceremony to be performed. He personally oversaw every aspect of the preparations, including running the rehearsal himself. He started by explaining to the other ministers how and when he would process into the church, how he would reverence the altar, and then, after he had been invested into his new clerical garb, how he would go over, kneel at the prie-dieu, and pause, as he explained, "as if to pray."

A similar story, this one true, a friend of mine told me because he was scandalized by what his friend had said to him. One morning, on the occasion of his friend's own fiftieth ordination anniversary, I believe, my friend was walking with him through the church toward the sacristy. People were coming in and taking their places in the pews. Some were praying the rosary; others were sitting quietly. The ministers were preparing the altar, lighting the candles and putting out the gifts. The choir was rehearsing. At the sacristy door, his friend turned, stretched out his hand to the devotion and activity of the faithful, and remarked, "Wouldn't it be great if it were all true?" This story was repeated to me many times, always with a kind of questioning. I suspect my friend kept telling the story of his friend, now deceased, trying to ascertain whether he had been joking or serious.

All of us have times when we feel like the protagonist in the Bob Fosse film *All That Jazz*. Burning the candle at both ends, a successful director is shown several times at the beginning of his day, splashing water on his face, putting drops into his bloodshot eyes, and popping uppers. Then, each time more beleagueredly, he announces to the face in the mirror, "It's show time!" Finally life does catch up to all of us, or will if it hasn't yet. Whether it was an emergency call to the hospital or a late-night card game, there come mornings when the last thing we feel like doing is leading scores of people in prayer. On those days, we go through the motions "as if to pray" as often as we actually do pray. We are saying the words of institution while thinking, with relief, that this liturgy will be done in no more than twelve minutes. Then we can get back to bed, or at least to coffee, just as long as no one corners us in the sacristy with a burning question of the day or an appeal for an impromptu confession. There are times, often for me during one or another of the great ethnic feasts of Our Lady, when a wave of cynicism comes over me. I look out at the sincere, passionate, but unevangelized throng and feel like whispering under my breath, "Wouldn't it be great if it were all true?"

When such feelings do not pass, when our cynical comments are not just the expression of a long day or a difficult task, when these feelings become our usual way of experiencing the world, we've contracted the affliction of acedia. We feel bad and bored at the same time, all our patterns and appetites and energies deranged. Dorothy Sayers describes it this way: "It is the sin that believes in nothing, cares for nothing, seeks to know nothing, interferes with nothing, enjoys nothing, hates nothing, finds purpose in nothing, lives for nothing, and remains alive because there is nothing for which it will die." John Cassian put a more positive spin on its ravages, saying that it comes upon us when "we have learned what we are unable to be, yet it has not made us be what we are striving to be." We are caught.

And we unwittingly catch others in our own web. A man told me of his experience with one of our pastors, a devoted priest and gentle soul. At the time, the fellow had been assigned as his "assistant." It was back in the days when an assistant was expected to be at meals and only to speak when spoken to (have times ever changed!). There were only the two of them then, as he tells it. At noon and at six exactly, they would meet at the dining room table, recite the Angelus together while the bells tolled, and then sit down and eat. The assistant said the two of them once went for an entire month, lunch and dinner, without the pastor once addressing a single word to him. Being Irish, the guy presumed he was being punished for something he had done that offended the pastor, and in the unforgiving silence, he had plenty of time to examine his conscience, desperate to determine which of his actions was responsible for the silent treatment.

As it turned out, it wasn't anything that this poor guy had done, though he could not have known it then. As he told me his story, I realized I had my own story of the pastor to tell. I was able to tell the assistant how someone had finally had the courage to sit down and have a heart-to-heart conversation with this pastor. Because of that chat, he sought help with his suffering. After so many years, he was diagnosed with clinical depression and very successfully treated. I reveal this story because I hear the priest's hoarse voice cracking toward me from the grave, "Tell them to get help if the dark clouds descend. I suffered for years needlessly." And so did many of his assistants and parishioners. If we wish to thrive in the future, we will need to provide one another stronger doses of frankness about depression and other forms of psychological illness.

Most cases of acedia are not so severe, although they are painful enough. No matter what we do or how successful we appear, we derive little pleasure or release from our activities. While we are resting, a disquieting anxiety and doubt can take hold; while active, the weight of depression often slows us down, as if we are trying to ford against a swift-moving stream. It's a little like being on steroids; you're tired and wired at the same time. Even our favorite vices can lose the kick they used to have to drown, release, deaden, or distract one from the idle restlessness. At times, it can become difficult to express oneself or follow a thought in writing. At parties, you feel like the one who has little to add to the conversations. As in hibernation, all the systems slow down.

It is important to recognize how different this is from grief. "In grief, the world becomes poor and empty," explained Freud, but "in melancholy, it is the ego itself" that becomes poor and empty. "Grief is depression," explains Andrew Solomon, "in proportion to circumstances; depression is grief out of proportion to circumstances." Someone you love dies or leaves the ministry; you grieve and you know why you feel so bad. "Grief is a humble angel who leaves you strong, clear thoughts and a sense of your own depth. Depression is a demon who leaves you appalled" because it often occurs without noticeable precipitants. That may be why Rufus of Ephesus described it as "a discreet aberration that occurred in otherwise stalwart minds." It deprives you of the very thing you need: the salt that used to give taste to your life.

†

The way many of us came to understand our calling and the way we were formed may exacerbate our bouts of acedia. What was going on when we started to take a priestly call seriously? Weren't many of us in our teens, even though our entrance into the seminary may have taken place years later? It happened to me during my adolescence in a burst of altruism. I think such altruism is one of the things that make teens so attractive. Like others of my age, I burned with ardent desire to work for the benefit of other people. Uncertain of, or untrusting in, his or her own native abilities, the young altruist is sustained by the pleasure of giving an all-embracing gift of self through an admirable group or cause. In nearly every generation, the young are the passionate revolutionaries and dedicated soldiers, the zealous monks and inventive professionals. Even parenting itself, at least at the beginning, is a great selfless surrender to the needs of one's child. Altruists believe that something extraordinary is possible, and for that they are willing to lose themselves.

Altruists consequently do not believe in half measures, and our formation tended to encourage us in this. I remember thinking that I wanted not simply to be a priest; I was determined to be a *great* priest. I aimed at being as spiritual as Thomas Merton, as dedicated as Dorothy Day, and as devoted as the charismatic younger priests I admired. With my friends, we were determined to be the ones who would make ourselves *ever* available; we would get to know *all* our parishioners and we would love them *unconditionally.*

It is a noble attraction, but untempered. Perhaps nothing revealed our immaturity so clearly as the common enemy we all despised, "the bastard pastor." He was what was wrong with the church. He went by many names, and we named them all. He was every priest we knew who took the wind out of our sails, those who would not let us do all the dramatic things we longed to do—the rock music at Mass, the "reach out" retreats with other youths, the homilies that entertained, the small groups of married couples who came together for spiritual discussions, all those conspicuous things that would make it clear that we were part of a new spirit, the untainted spirit of Vatican II with an energy unencumbered by the weight and excuses of the past. Like birds in flight, we loved the exhilaration, the thrill, the chance to escape gravity.

We turned out to be exactly what our parishioners wanted then in newly ordained priests. We were the ones who did the hospital calls, went over to the school, gathered the youth into service projects, and stayed after Mass to greet the people. We took the time to prepare our homilies and stayed after the baptisms as long as there was a photo left to take. We did not mind celebrating a number of Masses in a day or baptizing thirty babies at a crack; after all, we were part of something special. Bishops loved and still love such men, for they can be talked into difficult assignments, which they take and about which they do not complain. They will work long hours; they will skip days off and agree to all sorts of outside requests and added burdens; they will push themselves to the breaking point, sometimes past it.

One of the insidious pleasures of immature altruism is the illusion of being unaffected by such unlofty concerns as self-interest or any other lesser worries. Antiquity hailed as virtuous the person who was unaffected by normal feelings, that is, the one who was *apathetic.* Passions, particularly negative feelings, were what one strove to rise above. This was the Roman culture, not the Christian church, but Christian belief was deeply influenced by this dominant culture, or perhaps better, belief came to see itself through the lens of culture, as has happened in every other era, including our own.

Thus, when we read the lives of the ancient saints, we found stories of extraordinary men and women who were both ardent in act and perfectly in control of their passions, individuals who were never angry or let a mean thought cross their minds. These impervious ones would never hurt a fly or get an erection. The accounts of the martyrs' deaths, in particular, whether in paint or words, revealed the martyr's selfless and unaffected spiritual core. They seemed unmoved even by their own sufferings. Indeed many of the images of St. Sebastian gave the distinct impression that the young man actually enjoyed the sensation of arrows piercing his flesh. To the extent we believed such accounts, we felt not just justified but obligated to remain in the altruism of our adolescence. No, no, we were not becoming priests in order to be admired or for the respect that such a status would accord us. It was a sign of our dedication. We were not among those who counted the cost.

What these accounts of the saints left out, what they never revealed, was *how* the saints faced anything as natural as frailty, disappointment, loss, or sin—original or otherwise. That is why so many of us were unprepared when we came to the end of our altruism, when we started to realize with a shock—or have it shoved in our faces, like a protagonist in one of Flannery O'Connor's short stories—that we ourselves were not the saviors of anybody, that no one was printing up holy cards with our faces on them. We did not want to admit that we were indeed ordinary, tainted or worse, and that our motives were mixed and sometimes petty. How could we be the boring and intolerant fellows we vowed to defeat?

Let it be said that altruism has done a lot of good for the church. But the immaturity of it has also done a lot of harm.

As one gets a little older and the energy of one's youth declines, the untreated altruist can start to refuse to "do windows." He finds himself no longer eager to celebrate extra Masses on a Sunday, though he still believes he is saving the world. You won't find him sitting on the floor with the second graders or enduring the dull meetings of the parish council or school board. He can't be bothered to train the lectors or prepare the penance service. He disdains the efforts of "lesser" clergy, claiming to be "dedicating" himself to "real" ministry, which means those one or two special ministries for which he does manifest modest enthusiasm. Only these, says he, will change the world. He doesn't give the time of day to the people he sees outside of Sunday Mass, but he pours his heart out to those he meets giving a Marriage Encounter or through the Charismatic Renewal. His priesthood grows into a specialty: he gives himself not to others generally but to *these* others.

Thus does he convince himself that nothing is wrong. When he gets upset or cranky, it is never because he has lost his love for "the people." He continues to imagine himself invulnerable and grand even as the hole grows larger inside himself. He may even have scenarios to explain the barrenness he experiences in prayer.

In any honest life of a saint, you will find another story, one of lengthy struggle and much inner uncertainty. The two great Theresas, Ávila and the Little Flower, both seem to have suffered from depression, for example. Teresa of Ávila said she was burdened for years with barrenness in prayer, for which she made no excuses; later she succumbed to violent seizures and bouts of hysteria that eventually left her paralyzed, seized by the darkest visions. Unable to move, her pain was barely tolerable; at one point she was so deeply in a coma that her community dug her a grave. Then in

1540, she awoke and the paralysis was gone; she stood up and walked, a miracle.

The Little Flower's autobiography was so honest about her struggles that after her death her superiors covered over parts of it with a more circumspect and traditional accounting of a holy life. It was clear that at some point in her development she suffered something the equivalent of a nervous breakdown. This was not in spite of her spiritual life; it was *part* of her spiritual life. Depression affects one's functioning, not one's character.

An altruist thinks the world can be changed by impersonating Christ, meaning all his good qualities. This, he imagines, is what *in persona Christi* means. But normal human beings, mere disciples, come to recognize all good things as grace and even one's own virtues as gifts from God. In such circumstances, acedia is a gift, a necessary cure for adolescent immaturity through the painful but necessary unmasking of one's unexamined hubris.

This is why I love the unambiguous honesty of those desert rats at the end of antiquity. I never get tired of reading their stories, whose protagonists are strong but not at all impervious; the sayings detail the costs of discipleship clearly. They call a spade a spade, including, to echo contemporary concerns, the earliest direct warnings I have ever found about the danger of attachments to boys and the troubles of interacting with bishops.

The desert fathers say, "If you see a young man climbing toward heaven by his own will, grab his foot and pull him down, for it will be for his own good." This is not because only the old men have wisdom or because young men alone are afflicted with hubris. It is neither an age issue nor a control thing. Although Jesus gives his disciples lots to do, life is not what we *do;* it is what God *gives* us.

†

Because we tend to read the faith through the eyes of our own culture, many of us would automatically suppose that the spiritual life has, as its goal, psychological equilibrium. What your Lord wills is the same thing your shrink wants. This is not true, though, if the saints are any indication. Most of them have not been what you would call "Steady Eddies." They tended to be a bit high-strung or perhaps concentrated or moody. Many tended toward depression, particularly when they felt abandoned by God. Of all things, they did not expect "to feel good about themselves." They expected to be squeezed past themselves and their desires, to be drawn to something beyond their ken, and they prepared for it, often using the metaphor of battle. Often the communities in which they lived could not figure what to make of them except to acknowledge their sanctity.

Everyone who wants to deepen his or her spiritual life does not have to slip down into the dark cataract of major depression. But I do think that mild depression is a normal part of the spiritual life, especially in our middle years, and the wider recognition of this fact among us can lead to happier priests and better ministry. We have to get over the modern sense that, like never being angry or titillated, we are expected, and expect ourselves, never to be depressed. It's a fact of life and not necessarily a sign of moral weakness or underdeveloped virtue.

†

So what does one do about it? How does one pass by the dragon of *acedia* without being swallowed whole? (Here, besides sources from antiquity, I am indebted to Solomon's *Noonday Demon;*

his remedies are not theoretical but the fruit of his own struggle with bouts of acute depression.)

A key distinction helps you keep your bearings. The ascetics speak of "a right and useful grinding of the heart, which touches it deeply." This they contrast with a "grinding that is disorderly and harmful, which only leads to defeat." One grinding is to be embraced and the other is to be endured, in some ways overcome.

The right and useful grinding of the heart is the suffering that we bring on ourselves, as Sebastian Moore points out, "by our refusal to grow—by sin, in other words." In our middle years, we look back with less innocence and not a few bruises, and we see more clearly how we have failed or miscalculated or been unable to run away from certain things the way we believed we could. Mild depression can cause us to examine these aspects of our lives more closely. Acedia can act as the psychic equivalent of spring cleaning. We get so tired of things being the oppressive way that they are, we find the energy to clear the decks and often to redirect our energies in more useful ways. Perhaps this is a little of what hitting bottom means to an addict. We say to ourselves, "I can't possibly go on living this way," and so we go out and have that fight we needed to have with a superior, or find the courage to fire that troublesome staff member. We start that diet or ask a friend for a referral for counseling.

As with parents, there is a mighty press on priests to be just what is needed at the moment, to be only what our parishioners, staff, or bishop expect or need and not everything that we are. Sometimes we can be selfless in this way, but often we discover that we cannot, and don't really want to. Beset by depression, we sometimes are forced to actually go out and unbury a talent, to search and find a lost coin, to bring the lamp back out from under the sink.

Gifts that do not easily incorporate themselves into the rigors of our priestly lives are still gifts, and they may have an important, if as yet unseen, role to play in our lives or ministries. When a friend of mine complained of being depressed, someone in our support group reminded him of how much pleasure he took in playing the organ. He admitted that he had cast his musical talents aside in the name of being a good pastor, a dedicated priest, all that. Part of his restoration took place by his return to playing the organ.

This kind of growth and decision making needs to be embraced because it can lead us back to the experience of God in our lives. But a lot of acedia is what Amma Syncletica called "a grief that comes from the enemy, full of mockery." This is what needs to be endured, not embraced—even overcome in certain ways. Like enduring a fever that has to run its course, we sometimes get through mild depression simply by keeping up appearances. At times like these, love and friendship seem unreal, but somehow our vanity and sense of obligation do not fade. These can keep us going. "Strength of will is often the best bulwark against depression," Dr. Solomon warns. "If you push yourself too hard, you will make yourself worse, but you must push yourself hard enough if you really want to get out."

Perhaps this is why every abba and amma prescribed manual labor as part of the acedia's cure. Charlotte Brontë agreed: "Labour must be the cure, not sympathy—labour is the only radical cure for rooted sorrow." You aren't going to get better by just sitting there; you must keep moving. Exercise is our contemporary form of manual labor. I myself have never experienced those endorphins people claim kick in during exercise; sweat does not get me high. After exercise, all I am is tired. But the exertion does take the edge off the anxiety; it squeezes some of it out of me, and that helps.

†

Andrew Solomon says that the "most important thing to remember during depression is this: you don't get the time back...Even the minutes when you feel you are going to explode are minutes of your life, and you will never get those minutes again."

†

Often in acedia we come to recognize that we have been wasting our time on what's unimportant to us. Burnout, Paul Dudziak says, "comes from working too hard at tasks that matter too little." Burnout may indeed be the modern name for the "grinding that is disorderly and harmful, which only leads to defeat," for it leaves one in a state of unreasonable mental exhaustion. Amma Syncletica says that this "spirit must be cast out, mainly by prayer and psalmody." At first, one wonders how barren prayer, the kind that seems so utterly useless, can be of any help, but it is. Even when the words ring empty in my head and heart, a hidden power in ritual remains, which Brian Doyle calls "the skeleton that sustains us when we are weak." The very forms of prayer resonate off the walls and become, at the very least, an echo of a presence. Often I find in ritual a shape I can fit myself into; there, and nowhere else, I often find enough to keep going.

Presiding helps me too. Richard Rodriguez notes, "I was relieved of the burden of being alone before God through my membership in the Church." At times like these, I know what he means. I am grateful to be a Catholic; I could not abide having Jesus as just my own personal Lord and Savior; I require the church's support as much as anyone. Often enough I find myself in the midst of numbing days in which circumstances require me to celebrate three or four

Masses despite the dictates of canon law and the best advice of our spiritual advisors. On such occasions, if I let myself, I feel like one of those robots they have at Disneyland, an electronic character who gets up before each group to say exactly the same things in exactly the same way. I don't know where the real me goes, but he is far away. When I am also going through a period of depression or exhaustion, I feel anything but "into it." An altruist might view my actions as great selfless acts, the way I die to myself for the sake of the people I am serving. But if sacrifice is what is required of me, I prefer a different one. I challenge myself to enter the moment—to sacrifice *my* moment, the exhaustion or boredom I am feeling—for the lively mixture of feelings and sentiments that the congregation is feeling. I try to enter with them into the mysterious and almost untouchable presence of God. Without much myself, I try to find what's missing inside me and make what is theirs my own. I decide I can, at least for the next hour, set aside *my* circumstances for *our* prayer to the Father through Christ. I tell myself that my weariness or my preoccupations will be waiting for me in the sacristy after it is over, if I want to go back to them. This surrender is not an easy sacrifice; a halfhearted act of will leaves you feeling inauthentic and fraudulent. This is not a role you can put on for the sake of your performance. It does not work unless and until it becomes your prayer. I don't know exactly how it happens, but somehow the congregation and God uplift me. Though I start out dreading "show time," when I am confronted by everyone else out there, trying themselves to be present and pray, their praying often carries me; they change my mind; they persuade me, against my natural inclinations, to join them in prayer. Most comforting of all, God does bless the weary presider. When I look back, I realize that, at those grueling moments, I was given more of the grace God had for me than at any other time.

†

Don't imagine me docile at such times. If I were in John the Baptist's sandals, I would have gone to my beheading muttering, "Let me get this straight: I have to die because a cute teenager aroused a bunch of old drunks and her mother has an ax to grind?" That's the kind of helplessness I feel in acedia. To suffer for a noble and conspicuous cause, that would be tolerable; though unwelcome, I would be willing to die for my faith, but not for my emptiness.

It is humiliating to be vulnerable in this way, to feel trapped inside one's own soul. You have to have a kind of blind faith, a trust that within this unexplained misery there is some purpose and that enduring it is virtuous. Living by faith is not nearly as much fun as living by light. "For one is approved if, mindful of God, he endures pain while suffering unjustly," says St. Peter (1 Pet 2:19).

This is the other kind of suffering Sebastian Moore was talking about, a sharing in Christ's own suffering precisely because, like Christ's, it is undeserved. The undeserved suffering of acedia is part of being a creature, "subjected to futility," as St. Paul tells the Romans. With creation we await "with eager longing for the revealing of the sons of God." Jesus took up the cross to liberate us for those wonderful larger purposes of human life—for love, for forgiveness, for justice, for being instruments of God's peace—but only at God's *kairos* are we to be "free from…bondage to decay and obtain the glorious liberty of the children of God." Until then, we suffer in utter dependence on God.

†

A couple of times in Dr. Solomon's book, he mentions that societies "in transition" almost always have high levels of depression. Most of us live in such a society; in my own parish, almost everyone—priests and people—is from somewhere else, transplanted from the Philippines, Mexico, Korea, Nicaragua, Ireland, Vietnam, El Salvador, Kenya, and other places; some are even Anglos like me, who came to Orange County little more than a generation ago when the milk farms and orange groves were replaced by vast subdivisions. With so much change, we should not be surprised by how many more of us will experience acedia in one of its various forms. And certainly after the story of the scandals broke last year, if we had had any doubts about it before, our priesthood must also be considered a society undergoing dramatic and uncharted transition. If you are a little depressed, you have good reasons, and you are not alone.

†

As it drags on, remembering that acedia is just a passage helps. It is not life; it won't *always* feel this bad. My spinster great-aunt, a librarian in Los Angeles, suffered great bouts of depression. She was so bad she had to be given electric-shock treatments. After my grandmother died, there was no one in southern California but my sister and me to go and visit her in the hospital. I knew nothing about mental illness then, and so my visits to her were a terrible ordeal for me. She had delusions, believing that people were out to get her. I would try to reassure her that the orderly did not have a knife and was not trying to kill her for her money. He was just administering her medication. "That's what he says it is, medication, but…" I would interrupt her again with more reassurances, which would lead her to suspect that I too was now in a league with "them." It was a little like a scene from the film *A Beautiful Mind*.

Only once was I able to slice through the crippling haze of her projections. It was the last time she was hospitalized, as I recall, and I was preparing to leave after getting nowhere in our conversation. I don't know why I said what I said, perhaps out of frustration, but I asked her, "Aunt Ella, don't you remember? You were like this before. Just like this. And you got better."

"I was like this before?" she asked, unbelieving.

"Yes, it was a couple of years ago. I used to visit you, like I am doing now."

"And I got better?"

"Yes, you did. You were able to return to your apartment and go to Mass each morning at St. Basil's."

She withdrew into her mind for a moment, as if she vaguely remembered something like that possibly did happen once, long ago, almost as if in a former life. Then she came back to me and said, "I did, did I? That's good. That's good."

†

If you are going to fight for anything in acedia, fight with all your might to keep your sense of humor. That's the singing canary in the dark mineshaft of depression. With a sense of humor, you will recover. You will not get stuck. (In fact, I would say that the loss of one's sense of humor is the strongest indicator that one needs immediate professional help.) A sense of humor makes it a whole lot easier for your friends, staff, and family to love you and spend time with you. They can kid you about your anxiety or your complaints or your withdrawal, and you can kid them back. Most important, it's a lot harder for someone with a sense of humor to become self-indulgent. You are not just a man lost in your own soul; you are also someone looking at the guy lost in his own soul. You feel sorry for him, but you also laugh as he walks into walls and loses his place in the Eucharistic Prayer. He is pitiable, yes, but he is also pretty damn funny.

†

Like many people, I know someone who happened to be in New York on September 11, 2001. She was just four blocks from the World Trade Center when the first tower came down. She wrote to me of her harrowing experience of literally running for her life and having to find a way out of the city, back to her home hundreds of miles away. Once she got back there, she read the papers, followed the news, unable to get much else done as though she were still in the swirling dust cloud. I wrote her a note to say that I was praying for her, and did not hear from her again until she sent me a card sometime in the spring. In it, she reported a surprising renewed sense of joy despite the fact that a dear friend was suicidal. She said she told her friend she'll "be dead soon enough, we all will," but "until then there are just a few minutes to look and see what is in front of us." She ended her letter by saying, "The truth is I'm happy. I take enormous pleasure in the flowering trees and the return of every small bird that took off for Florida last fall…The dog is snoring under the desk. It's as much as anyone could want." If there is a purification in acedia, it is something like this: we come to recognize as precious what we might previously have taken for granted or not noticed at all, God's loving mercy most of all. Léon Bloy put it in a slightly different way: "There are places in our hearts which do not yet exist, and it is necessary for suffering to penetrate there in order that they may come into being." Acedia endured can help us recognize that we live, despite the rigors, in a universe of wonders.

—⟋⟋⟋—

It is true that the unknown is
the largest need of the intellect,
although for this no one thinks to thank God.

EMILY DICKINSON

—⟋⟋⟋—

THE TRUTH
THAT WILL
SET YOU FREE

If for nothing else, Pontius Pilate is remembered for his question "What is truth?" (John 18:38). On Good Friday, the question is generally proclaimed with a disparaging voice, implying that Pilate will not be distracted by anything as paltry or ineffectual as truth. I take John to be unsympathetic to Pilate, so such a reading may be the evangelist's intent. But nothing in the fourth gospel is only what it seems; the word *truth* appears nineteen times in this gospel while only four times in all of the Synoptics. Truth is important to its message, for it is what John tells us Jesus promised would set us free (John 8:32). I expect it is not the kind of question a young man would ask. Am I reading too much into it when I hear his question as that of a man of experience not wishing to become cynical? Pilate's question is, after all, a good question, at least for me at this point in my life and in "the present climate." A little freedom would be welcome right now, don't you think?

†

Who knew, when they went to church on a particularly sleepy Sunday morning, that the droning preacher would get so fired up, that he would say his first passionate words in four years? To everyone's surprise, including his own, he raises his voice. He says, "We must forgive! We absolutely must!" And who could have predicted the blaze these few demanding words would inflame in the congregation? Certainly not Barbara, who had no idea she was going to return home from church that morning and make a phone call, right away, before she lost her courage. When she got up in the darkness and dressed for the early Mass, she did not see herself dialing the number of someone she had come to hate—and hate, she felt, for many good reasons. The last thing she imagined she would hear herself say that day, when finally the phone was answered, was, "Mom? It's Barbara. I called to say I am sorry."

Her statement is not a simple one. To the newspaper, the reconciliation of mother and daughter may be a heartwarming story, I suppose, worthy of the lifestyle section. But this phone call complicates the lives of Barbara and her mother, of course, because it creates more truth between them, truth that is confusing at first because it goes against what both have believed and that will have to be sorted out in future conversations. Although it could be lost if they slip back into their bickering ways, these words of apology might just be the truth that sets them free from their old habits and heals their wounds; it could lead to forgiveness, understanding, reconciliation, even to new life.

The truth that sets one free is, in my experience, a revelation, something almost always unexpected but longed for, often in unconscious ways. That's why you immediately recognize it for what it is.

Yet, at first glance, this truth is frequently unwelcome, a bit scary really, making you unsure, as it does, of what you had previously been so confident. It does not coerce you, but it does stand forcefully on its own two feet, waiting for you to respond. It is something that, once stated, changes the ways you have known and lived your life, even if you reject its invitation. Its freedom is precisely what makes it so strong. It is an open door. Dare you enter?

If, as Cardinal Suhard has said, "one of the priest's first services to the world is to tell the truth," how do we come upon this kind of truth? Do we simply hope to receive the occasional lucky gift from above? A friend of mine says, for example, that when preparing to preach, we should pray for the grace to say to these particular people what God wants them to hear on this particular Sunday; we should pray for accuracy, hoping that our words express a revelatory truth. But I think our whole lives ought to be lived so as to dispose ourselves to receive such inspirations. Accuracy requires a sharp eye, a talent for looking hard at how, in this world of ours, life really is. And not just life in general. Through much listening, questioning, conversation, and immersion into the lives of our parishioners, we see the contours in detail; it is *their* lives, of course, that we hope to touch. Here Aquinas was particularly correct: revelatory grace does build on perceptive human nature. But we also have to go as far as we can inside ourselves to hear that revealing voice. To be accurate, one needs study and reflection, knowledge and self-knowledge. It is not a knack; it is a gift that comes only to those who really work for it.

I've learned a lot about this from my friend John Sammon, who is celebrating his sixty-fifth priestly anniversary this year. He was always a bit of a maverick, getting under the skin of Cardinal McIntyre for being involved in civic affairs by taking an interest in the police, the firemen, the scouts, even local politicians. From the very beginning, he was one of those priests who never let the fact that some people weren't Catholic get in the way of his ministering to them. When there is an emergency, especially if an officer or fireman has been killed or injured, John has been the one they call first because they are sure that he'll know how to help everyone cope; he'll know what to say; with him around, everyone will start to believe that they'll get through all this. In their suffering he is their witness, their confidant, and their intercessor. He has figured out how to be holy without being predictable or sounding the least bit pious, which makes him by far the most popular preacher in our diocese. His down-to-earth, often humorous invocations and blessings are much appreciated. More than any other person I know, he is likely to speak the freeing truth.

Those of us who know him know two things. One, he is a very busy priest, perhaps slightly slowed of late because of his years and because he had to give up driving but still very much involved in the myriad forms of his ministry. And the other thing we know is that he reads a lot, a tremendous lot, and has done so for as far back as any of us can remember. There's a connection here between his immersion in the lives of the people he serves and his immersion in the wisdom and vitality he finds in his books. At times he seems to be everywhere at once, but visit his room and you will see his volumes; they are stacked three and four deep on the shelves, and the titles show his very wide interests. He has been busier than any of us, but when he gets home or before he goes out, he is reading—no—he is *absorbing* his books. You hear it behind everything he says. I don't know how he does it, but it is something I try to emulate. In head and heart, in thought and life, one sees in John an unwavering and absolute dedication to the truth that sets one free. He'll hunt it down wherever he can find it. And for that effort, he has been rewarded with the capacity to pack and then unpack the mind and heart with words. At the needed moment of crisis or celebration or prayer, he's been unfailingly able to say the right thing, to voice the revealing truth.

I offer him as an antidote to the anti-intellectualism for which we parish priests have too often prided ourselves. Some of us gloat about how we have not cracked a book since the seminary and won't even bother to do those quickie one-day workshops the diocese puts on. Under duress, we'll scan the occasional article or submit to diocesan-mandated study days (especially if they are taking attendance), but we protest that everything priests need to know can be learned in the parking lot and the confessional. We are the guys in the streets, it is argued, not theoreticians perched in some think tank. To me, this is a completely specious contention, as the life of someone like John Sammon shows.

Ours is not a turnkey operation, not anymore. What's expected of us is complicated and wide-ranging and multifaceted, and getting more so every day. It touches almost every aspect of life. Yes, we are often bureaucrats charged with worry about the lights, locks, leaks, loot, litter, and liability—especially liability these days. But we also direct the spiritual and moral formation of adults, the upbringing of children in the ways of the faith, the organization and direction of many intersecting groups, the management of often tight finances and the fund-raising it requires. We explain the scriptures, pass on the tradition and history of the church, and facilitate the conversion of souls, not to mention fielding frequent questions and doubts about the meaning of life and human destiny. We do these things on a regular basis. I cannot imagine surviving the priesthood today without trying to be as smart and experienced as one possibly can.

†

What might be the freeing truth that we ourselves now need as a priest*hood,* as a presbyterate? Over the years, I have met a lot of priests around the country and visited a number of dioceses. Yes, we have our complaints about one another; like brothers in a big family, we are always pointing out one another's faults. Among the priests I know, though, most do genuinely care about their confreres. It is obvious in the way we greet one another and take time to catch up with one another, in the way we are willing to put ourselves out to help one another in our parishes, and especially in the way we pray together and laugh with one another on occasions of retreat and convocation.

As welcome as all this is, I think we have gone about as far as we can go through polite conversation and friendly collaboration. What we have is good and helpful, but I have the feeling that we need something more, a greater transparency or openness or honesty, whatever you want to call it. If ever there was, it is now time to voice greater truth among us.

There are a number of reasons I feel this way. First, we are quickly becoming a different priesthood than we were, a fact we sometimes overlook. The next time you gather, look around. We are many fewer, of course, and in the cases where we still have hair, ours is more likely to be gray than blond or brown or black. Moreover, those who have been ordained in recent years are men of very different experiences, often coming from very different backgrounds and formations. They did not have the benefit of twelve or eight years getting to know one another in the seminary; sometimes they had as little as four years. Most come to the priesthood after experiences in business or the military or after immigrating from distant parts of the world. Without knowing each other sufficiently, how will we really be a body?

†

I have long been convinced that our strength comes from being a body. This notion that priests are "independent agents" has no justification in our history, or canon law, for that matter. The presbyterate was originally and is today, before all else, a college, a specific order in the church. Long before we ever celebrated a Mass, anointed a body, or chaired a meeting, we were the advisors gathered as a body around the bishop. We rightly pride ourselves on not being monks and not wanting to live like monks—a point I wholeheartedly agree with—but it is an indisputable fact that centuries before Benedict ever thought of banding together the eccentric hermits living around Subiaco, we were already a union. Unlike religious communities who witness to the evangelical virtues, the presbyterate did not and does not now exist as a witness to anything in particular, a point I promise to get to eventually, nor does it cloister itself apart from the local church. With the other orders—the baptized, the deacons, the catechumens, and the penitents—we gather at the altar as a priest*hood* around our bishop.

†

The sense of a common presbyterial life and practice, I fear, is fading among us. More and more, we don't even live together—a situation, I admit, that has its advantages—but I sense the air leaking out of our enthusiasm to know one another better even when opportunities do arise. If you've been going to priests' retreats long enough, you have probably had this experience of déjà vu: you are sitting at breakfast; a priest whom you know in passing sits down with his plate of scrambled eggs, and the two of you talk about, well, what the two of you talked about last year—or was it the year before?—when you happened to find yourselves sitting together with similar plates of eggs. You talk about what you know *about* him. You ask about his parish, or his recent move, or whatever little bit of news you already know about him. How about all those things we *don't* know about each other's lives? Ask about that and we just might hear truth that will set us free.

Most of us have been brought up as men of honor. We tell the truth. Like George Washington, we will not tell a lie. But that's limited to facts. When it comes to our own feelings, we remain inveterate liars. That kind of honesty has not been considered important among us or, worse, is a sign of weakness. When someone asks me, "How's it going?" I don't even stop to ask myself what I am feeling. I answer, "Fine," or even, "Great!" without thinking. How I'm feeling is not important, not even to me. Besides, I tell myself that you don't want to know, not really. I keep quiet to spare your feelings. At least this is my excuse, a white lie I tell myself while claiming it is for your benefit. Why should I burden you with my troubles? You don't really want to know, do you? Aren't these kinds of things best kept to ourselves? A selfless priest does not wear his heart on his sleeve; he has no time for such petty things as feelings.

Well, actually, no, I don't think we should keep our feelings to ourselves, especially now. Wouldn't it be helpful for us to talk about what is "at stake" in our lives. One of the reasons I am writing these essays is in the hope of hearing how the recent crisis is affecting you, a priest like me. Are you depressed? Do you feel betrayed? Are you defiant or just plain tired? Do you wish the whole damned thing would go away? Myself, I am tired of having to check the newspaper each morning to find out what kind of a day it is going to be. Is that how you feel? Or would you like to change the subject and talk about anything else? Do you remember when all we had to worry about was organizing the confirmation retreat and increasing our Sunday collections? I miss those days.

At a time of crisis, people often find the freedom to voice things they ordinarily would not express. A dying woman can give advice to her children; a soldier going off to war can tell his brother that he loves him dearly; a father can talk with his daughter about fear and worry and faith as he prepares for a dangerous surgery. As men who have suffered as many hits as we have in the last couple of years, we priests can pretty much talk about whatever we want and in whatever way we want to talk about it. We've earned the right.

†

There's the very real danger of conflict, of course. You and I may not like the way the other sees things. I hear through the grapevine that you've taken to wearing a cassock on Sundays, and you hear rumors that I am enthusiastic about a theologian you suspect of heresy. Someone told me your big project went down in flames, and you hear that I have become as hard as nails. These are the very things we have trained ourselves never to mention. But how strong is a bond that is never risked? What kind of brothers are we if we dare not ask or respond honestly for fear of disagreement? You can't know how deep the waters are until you dive into them.

I offer the example of Michael Duffy and myself when we were assigned together. Though we became friends, that came only after we fought. Our first big donnybrook was over a little church key. Michael had taken it away from the sacristan for doing something that he didn't like. The fight started because he found out that I had returned that key to the sacristan. He was hopping mad and told me as soon as we sat down to dinner that night. Why, he wanted to know, had I done this without his permission? I told him I returned the key because I thought he was being petty—that and the fact that, without the sacristan having a key, I was sick and tired of having to go over to open the church each time I had the early Mass. After our opening salvos, there was no stopping us. We were quite ugly, both of us voicing everything that had ever disturbed us about the other, fighting as dirtily as we possibly could. Neither was interested in truth, certainly not understanding or resolution; each of us simply wanted to vanquish the other. I can't remember how it ended. Since neither of us was prepared to give an inch, I imagine it ended only when one of us was called to our evening appointment. When I think of my behavior that night, I still blush.

Afterwards, I was convinced that Michael would call the diocese first thing in the morning to ask to have me reassigned. Instead, what happened was that we became friends. I am not sure how it happened—we had many more, though more focused, less ferocious, fights—but I think the confrontations, in an odd way, helped us along the way. The exchanges meant, at least, that we took seriously what the other thought or believed to be true. (We eventually learned to listen to the other's point even while insisting on our own.) You dismiss what and whom you don't care about, but you fight for what matters to you and you fight with those whose lives have some standing with you. The last time I ran into Michael Duffy, only a couple of weeks before the accident that ended his life, he brought the fighting up to me, telling me how grateful he was that I showed him how you could fight and still be friends. But I had always believed it was the other way around. In my family, we aren't fighters; we are withdrawers. I always thought that it was Michael who taught me that you could fight and still be friends.

In our society, it is believed that challenging someone's opinions, beliefs, or assumptions or having someone challenge ours is somehow an act of violence or disrespect, an attempt to undermine a person's "reality." This abandonment of anything approaching the objective is very disturbing because it leaves each of us free to create our own reality, a reality no one has the right to challenge. Out of this spring enthusiastic consumers, single-minded terrorists, and clueless narcissists. It allows people to disregard the fact that we share in common the same light, air, and earth, that we are a species interlinked by DNA, histories, culture, languages, poetry, and the responsibility for the future of life on this planet.

Our Catholic tradition takes an opposite tack. When the medieval theologians debated, they were not motivated by the desire to win, to beat their opponent (at least the best of them weren't). They wanted to demonstrate what was true and unmask what was in error. Theirs was the search for honest utterance among people, not individual reality. In a time when reality means anything from the personal to the virtual, we need that more now than they ever did.

†

The most important reason for us to try to speak the freeing truth to one another is that it is what we need to thrive. I think all of us, except the recently ordained, have had this experience: We've known a priest pretty well. We were assigned with him or came to know him through a support group or by working together on one or another board or committee, a man who seemed fine to us. We thought of him as just one of the guys. If we noticed anything over the years, it was that he looked more tired than usual or a bit more withdrawn. He started skipping those deanery meetings he used to attend. And then the word gets out that he has left the active ministry or that he is on administrative leave because of some charges made against him; we learn that he has had a breakdown, or that he was the subject of an intervention, or any number of circumstances that removed him from our midst as if in the middle of the night.

These are the men who used to be members of the presbyterate and are not now. I don't know how many you know, but in my diocese there are many. I served with a priest who was later convicted of child molestation. My classmate took a leave of absence, as did a member of my support group. A friend of more than thirty years had to resign his parish amid allegations of sexual misconduct with teens. And just recently, my parochial vicar took a leave of absence after only four years in the ministry. I am not suggesting a direct connection between the spirit of a presbyterate and what happened to these brothers. Life is, of course, very complicated. Who can know if things could have worked out any differently for any of them? But one thing is likely: whatever it was that they needed, esprit was not it, not by a long shot. Only stronger bonds and deeper and more honest truth will be tough enough to do us, as a presbyterate, any real good.

†

About a year ago, I noticed an article in the newspaper about a fifty-five-year-old priest who had committed suicide. He had been serving fifteen hundred parishioners in three parishes. I did not know him but was saddened by the news, of course. But I was also astonished by the comments reported as being made by his vicar general. "Priests, as a group, are people who are willing to work hard," he told the press. "We have our share of workaholics. We'd like it if they were more reasonable about living a healthy lifestyle."

Besides being an absolutely patronizing way of covering over the tragic death of a brother priest, he did what we priests tend to do too often: he spoke in the third-person plural. He spoke of his brother priest from a distance, and a judgmental one at that. He spoke of "priests as a group" and "workaholics" rather than "Mark." I would have liked to hear an expression of his feelings of loss, or anger that such a terrible thing occurred, or regret that he didn't do something in time to keep this from happening to this poor priest.

Please, let's stop speaking of one another in that way. I'm all for respecting the boundaries, but respecting the boundaries should not be used as a pretext for keeping one's distance. If you think I'm losing it, don't wait until I go out, buy a pistol, and aim it at my head. Instead of giving a press conference after my demise, come over, talk to me directly as soon as you hear, even at the risk of losing me as a friend. This is without doubt truth that can set one free.

This is harder than it sounds, much harder. It takes the kind of courage that most of us don't have. We spend our workouts on the *friendly* muscles; we bench-press those we use all the time, the ones that help us be *nice,* the ones we use to be very *agreeable.* Telling it like it is? No, we aren't so practiced at that.

A few years ago I went on a vacation with a couple of my friends. By day we had a wonderful time, but one of my friends got himself really plastered each evening. I don't know if he was drinking in the afternoon when we were napping, but he became utterly useless for conversation or anything else after sundown. Since eating a good dinner is one of my favorite things, he nearly ruined the trip for me, though I didn't say anything about it to him at the time, of course. Later, when he broached the idea of planning our next wonderful trip, I took a deep breath, then another, and finally said that I wasn't interested in repeating the embarrassed scenes from the previous trip. I told him he was fun to travel with but only up to seven in the evening. When he asked me what I was talking about, I reminded him of the behaviors that upset me, though I am not sure he remembered them himself; he seemed stunned, as though I were talking about someone else. Of course, it meant that our friendship was never the same again. That conversation created more truth between us, truth that complicated our lives and that we are still trying to sort out. Sometimes one of us loses his nerve and we go back to our old silent ways. But we are gaining a great deal by our honesty, perhaps even a truth that will set us both free. These kinds of risk are the ones we need to take with one another if we are hoping to be more than hail-fellows-well-met.

I suspect the regular practice of speaking more honestly with one another will make the need for interventions and confrontations less necessary, since we won't wait to speak up until a situation becomes untenable. We might even get to the point of initiating conversations: *I can tell you're upset. You want to tell me what the problem is?* You'll mention what I had not noticed, that in my voice there's a certain new hardness. I'll ask you why you always seem so sad nowadays. Though I wished you didn't say it, I'll know that you are right when you tell me that it is high time for me to apologize for my most recent tantrum. We'll both think twice about our words and behaviors if we know the other will confront us about them when we are out of line. More honesty in conversation will make it harder for each of us to hide from ourselves or from the consequences of our actions or inactions. It will be harder, yes, but that will also make it better.

†

Honesty is not just for confrontations, of course. It can just as easily express the kind of respect and appreciation that can really make a difference. If I know you'll tell me when I'm wrong, I might just believe you when you tell me that I am doing something right, when you, who do the same job as I, tell me that I am doing very good work. This can set us free because we all learn much faster when we are told what we're doing *right* rather than by being told what we're doing *wrong*. Two examples:

One summer, my father got it into his head that if I was going to become a priest, I needed to learn how to play golf. This was not a suggestion open for discussion; this was his conclusion. So each Sunday afternoon for a month, he took me out to the driving range and I hit a bucket of balls. My dad would watch and tell me what I was doing wrong; each swing was an opportunity for me to learn what *not* to do. Since this didn't tell me what I *should* do, at the end of the month my swing was actually worse than when I started. My father gave up. I contrast this with hitting a bucket of balls with friends a couple of years ago when we had an hour to kill before the Chrism Mass. They were golfers; I was just tagging along. When I did something right—still an unanticipated occurrence—they would say, "Did you feel that? Did you feel how that swing worked so much better?" They taught me what works by showing me what I was doing *right*. A word of honest appreciation can make a big difference, especially when someone is trying to do something difficult.

Another Michael Duffy story, this one about his first assignment. He was way out in rural Santa Maria County, I think, with a very tough pastor. Michael told me that life with him was miserable until he received an unexpected call from one of the auxiliary bishops, who asked him to meet him at a nearby convent. Michael, of course, thought he was in trouble, but that was the opposite of the bishop's intent. Michael was stunned when the bishop told him that he and the archbishop wanted him to know that they knew his pastor was not the easiest guy to live with. They recognized how very demanding he could be. This was why they appreciated Michael for trying to do his best to get along with him. The bishop even thanked him for his effort. Well, after that, Michael told me, he could have stayed in that assignment for a million years. He had heard the truth that set him free.

Here's another reason. I thought of it when we had a long discussion about vocations a couple of months back at our Council of Priests. For once we stopped talking like elected officials or midlevel managers; we spoke with the hearts of shepherds, sounding for all the world like parents worried about the future of their families. We spoke not just about the "problem" but how we felt and what we hoped for despite discouraging prospects. I sensed that many of us would enjoy more such thoughtful and affecting conversations among us. Not more meetings, God save us, but more common leadership.

As an institution, we need to have clear lines of responsibility, appropriate ministry descriptions, and the like. In many ways, divide does conquer. *You take the Spanish. I'll do the R.C.I.A. And let's trade off doing the youth Mass.* This is the pastoral side of things, and we are good at it because of such distinctions. Yet when it comes to what would be good for my parish and for our local church, I would rather work and reflect and decide with others. Collaboration has many faults, not the least of which is the enormous time it requires to hear everyone out and, when possible, to reach a consensus, but its redeeming virtue is a shared vision, even solidarity, especially when the words that are spoken come not only from practicality or a certain theoretical framework but from experience and from what we discover in our hearts as a result of our experiences.

A flock has to be going somewhere, and sooner or later even servant-leaders must lead. Many of us are doing this in our parishes through parish councils and other advisory bodies. We don't do this, at least not sufficiently, as a presbyterate. In my diocese, we left leadership more or less to our bishops, a situation that seemed to suit them just fine. But pause for a moment and you'll notice something if your diocese is anything like mine. Our ordinaries have all come from somewhere *else,* and without surprising changes in the ways bishops are appointed, future ordinaries are likely to come from somewhere else too. I say this not as a criticism but as a reality, a fact. It is not necessarily always a bad thing, but who will know and tell the outsider what grows in our particular pastoral fields? Isn't this really, in large measure, the job of a presbyterate? After all, our original and single responsibility was to advise the bishop.

†

One night years ago, at our House of Prayer for Priests, I was sitting out on the patio after dinner with a Jesuit friend, wandering from topic to topic, as is sometimes our custom. Somehow we got into a discussion about the difference between religious and diocesan priests. As far as I could see it, I told him the fundamental difference was between witness and work. Religious take on their promises or vows of poverty, chastity, and obedience as an evangelical witness, a sign of the heavenly kingdom in this world. We parish priests make promises, as is clear in the way we are ordained, for the sake of the ministry we have been given. Fundamentally, we are not witnesses but ministers. He countered that religious often take on apostolic works. Even monks take parishes and run educational institutions. The Jesuit formation is in many ways the opposite of the monastic, he pointed out, since it trains a companion of Jesus to live, pray, and work without a lot of community support. He was right about that, of course. "How are your pastoral efforts so different from the Jesuits'?" he asked.

It was and is a good question. My answer that night was that our stake was *territorial*. We are not devoted to a worthy goal, such as care for the poor or spiritual formation; we are devoted to the people who live in one particular place, to the flock envisioned as a diocese. About this place we aim to be experts.

We are, therefore, more like farmers than explorers. An explorer takes the macro view, wanting to be conversant with the wide outlines of the known world by travel and scrutiny of the far frontiers. The micro view is narrow, like the intelligence of a skilled vintner who knows what grapes will grow on what hillsides, which need irrigation and which need to be stressed. Parish priests and farmers stay home and peer closely at what's around us, wanting to know everything about this one place. They seek to know what will and will not grow here and, through experiment and long experience, to make what does grow here do better. I'm not sure that I convinced my Jesuit friend that night, but I offer it as a way of looking upon our priestly leadership. Though we ourselves certainly have no corner on the truth, we ought to be collaborators with all who can help us understand this place and these peoples and the signs of these times. From the earliest days, one of the key tasks of any presbyterate has been to discover what specific truth will set free these people, these parishes, and this local church.

†

In most places, the pastoral problems we face as fishers of men and women revolve around the wondrous catch's strain on our nets and on us, a shrinking workforce, who have to keep hauling in the fish. How shall we continue to find the strength to keep working the nets except together? If we allow our communities to divide us into the conservative and the liberal, or the Hispanic and the Anglo, or within our ethnic communities into those who favor assimilation (usually the younger generation) and those who want to protect the old country ways (usually the older generation), what will happen? And if we allow a division between the parishes that can afford good ministry and those that can't, or if each of us gives himself *only* to those ministries for which he personally has enthusiasm—you racing off to your death penalty vigil and I to a conference on the arts, another spreading the spirituality of the Legion of Mary while someone else attends the liturgy study days—what will happen? We shall find ourselves still working very hard, and we shall surely have our sectarian supporters and admirers, but I believe we'll be lonely priests, returning after all these diverse efforts to rattle around our big old rectories. When forced by circumstance to meet, we'll come to peer at one another with vague disgust and growing suspicion.

We enjoy a certain refuge when we make decisions together and support each other in them. I am as tired as anyone with the "norms" that come down to us from the diocese, but there is something to be said for our liturgies as well as our pastoral practices remaining within certain ranges. Although it is somewhat flattering to discover that scores of people are coming over to your parish from the neighbor because they love your liturgies or your preaching or your whatever, the thrill soon wears off. More people are more work. These new people often have less of a commitment to your parish than their compliments suggest. They love you for what you can do for them. What do you think will happen on the day you don't do what they want? They can be like the rich people Ernest Hemingway complained about: "the good, the attractive, the charming, the soon-beloved rich who have no bad qualities and who give each day the quality of a festival; when they have passed and taken the nourishment they needed, they leave everything deader than the roots of any grass Attila's horses hooves have ever scoured."

I don't believe we are condemned to bland uniformity from parish to parish or to policies that reflect nothing but the least common denominator, though this is what we have come to expect in some places. Rather, it is to our advantage and remains our difficult task to find the more complicated truth—past the shallow, the narrowly orthodox, and the merely trendy. We've seen so many of these kinds of things come and go, aren't we ready to find and commit ourselves to the lasting practices, the trustworthy paths that can set this *and* the next generation free, this community *and* all the others too, this parish *and* the whole diocese?

†

Those among us and in our dioceses who wish to divide us often do so in the name of truth, and should we question their views, they are quick to accuse us of having no guts or of complicity with forces opposed to the church or the Holy Spirit. They charge us with going against the intentions of Vatican II or of the Holy Father. The truth they describe is something small and practical, a tool like a screwdriver, a thing that answers their need, or fits into a course of action they find attractive, or satisfies a problem they are worked up over. It is *a* truth, clearly defined, sharp as a scalpel. Even among the traditionalists, many find the sophistication of our beliefs too subtle, a trifle too complicated and baroque for their tastes. They worry about too much wiggle room and too much to think about. In our fast-paced world, they prefer a simple truth, a concluding truth, a truth that can be set out on a single page of 8 $\frac{1}{2}$-by-11-inch paper. They want only the simple songs, those easy enough to memorize, melodies that comfort the heart rather than tax the intellect. In almost every society, religion, and culture, people all across the globe seem to be racing eagerly toward the sound bite and headline-clarifying singleness of vision of the fundamentalist. Perhaps this is in reaction to the cacophonous blare of globalization. In the end, they may win the day.

Still, as a Catholic, I ask what's the point of building libraries, issuing documents and decrees, holding synods and councils? Why bring thousands of the most sophisticated people together in colleges and universities if all you want is the outline version? Why expend so much effort in our parishes with expectations for sacramental preparation and training for catechists and ministers if black and white is good enough? Why work so hard to keep your school open and your enrollment up if all you want is conformity on a few worrisome issues? Why support so many cultures and ways of seeing things? Why have something as complicated and as beautiful as the whole Bible when all you want to do is keep people in line?

The truth that sets people free is so capacious that we have to walk around it many times to take in all its facets and dimensions. It consists of a glorious and intricate specificity, and anyone who tells you otherwise has never really experienced it. It is as wide as the created universe and as specific as the person of Jesus. To name such truth is the task of tradition, and it takes centuries of contemplation and discriminating thought to find it.

Yes, simple fishermen, prostitutes, and tax collectors were able to understand Jesus, though not always easily or quickly. There's always one or another disciple with a hand up, wanting to ask a question. Yes, Jesus might have made our task a lot easier had he explained his teachings in a letter, like St. Paul, or in a creed, like the fathers of the church, or in a theological treatise, like Thomas

Aquinas or Karl Rahner, or in a catechism, like Trent, or in manuals of devotion, like à Kempis or de Sales, or in fiction, like Mauriac or Walker Percy, or poetry, like John of the Cross or Gerard Manley Hopkins, or memoir, like Thomas Merton or Henri Nouwen. The scriptures have been written in all these genres because Jesus meant his truth to be known in and through every means of revelation there is.

Perhaps Jesus preferred to speak in parables to keep his truth from immediately being set in stone, memorized, or owned. He expected his disciples to have to chew on them a while to unlock their flavor. It was not a lesson we learn easily. Even the inspired evangelists could not resist playing the interpreter. Mark did the least editorializing. But when Matthew and Luke reported Jesus' parables, they added to them their own moral (Luke) or midrash (Matthew). They clearly wanted to make sure the hearer wouldn't get the wrong idea. Instead of parables, John has many dazzling metaphors that seem to serve the same purpose: to keep mystery in truth, and revelation in experience.

Since we are pastors, ours is not to decide which one thing is really important but to discern the Spirit's direction in all the truth there is, to honor everything that deepens and enlarges our understanding of the riddle of life. What we contemplate must match the splendor of creation itself, possessing, to use Francis Fergusson's lovely phrase, "all the sights and sounds and smells of 'God's world!'" Jesus' words and life are a revelation for everyone and a mystery enfolding each one. His transforming truth complicates our lives, of course, because we have to wrestle with it and change our ways in response to it. Through it, we build up the walls of the church with definitions and tradition; we build them as tall as we can, cementing the stones with quotations from the scriptures, the fathers, the councils, theologians, and the prayers of every holy person. "Far from being what is left over after theology has done its best, mystery is the very substance on which theology feeds and thrives," explains Avery Dulles. "A statement free from mystery would hardly be, in the proper sense, theological." Since our eyes are still gazing heavenward, we leave the roof open. We contemplate truth as something that can be contained and specified, and yet every formation of it remains incomplete, something we both believe in and live as an open-ended question. As Marilynne Robinson explains, "A question is more spacious than a statement, far better suited to expressing wonder."

THE NEAR ENEMIES

"The great temptation is to be a bureaucrat of the sect and not a priest of the whole mystery," the retreat master proclaimed. "The great sin is infantilism." I had never heard the word before; I had to look it up. The speaker was the renowned theologian, Raimundo Panikkar, a man whose words were to be taken seriously, I presumed, but how exactly do adults act like babies and in what way was that a peril? I had no answer back then as I was preparing for ordination, but his words have haunted me over the years. When so many other thoughts have been lost, why did this statement stick on my memory? I think it is because, in myself and in others, I keep bumping into examples of the very childish behavior he was so worried about. I worry about it too.

We fret that the church is going to ask too much of us, but the danger here comes when the church asks too little. In her great and successful institutionality, she has an undeniable preference for the shapely cog that fits nicely into that tiny little gear inside the well-oiled machine. Like harried mothers, the church takes advantage of those who are useful in small matters, those who can get the work done and on time, those who are accommodating and easy to direct.

Thus, too often she favors those who are predictable and practical, the sectarian over the mystic, the organizer over the dreamer, the bureaucrat over the sage, even, I fear, the pious over the saint. As I mentioned earlier, many of those who moved the church forward were rewarded for their efforts with suspicion and distrust from small-minded leaders in the church. In conscious and unconscious ways, the church prefers less than the best we have to offer.

Before we get on our high horse, let us remember that when we speak of the church, we are not talking about somebody else out there. Though we prefer an image of ourselves as mavericks on the frontiers, parish priests are about as institutional as it gets. We are local leaders and pretty powerful in our precincts. And on our own turfs, we too can favor usefulness over vision. We have jobs that have to be done, and we find ourselves honoring those who, we know, can help us get them done. We all know how to be near-sighted when we need to, and thereby we can encourage a comfortable narrowness among our collaborators.

To accept this state of affairs or, worse, to adopt its pragmatic modesty as a kind of guide for one's behavior, as I have seen done, is an example of infantilism. In time, one becomes content with the mere fulfillment of obligations or modest expectations; like a trained pet, we are well fed and so we perform our tricks. We stop looking up from our bowl.

This is one reason so few of us really excel. How many of us are holy, for example? I fear too many of us don't even try very hard anymore to become holy. I'm not blaming the church. I'm a big boy and rarely have I had someone actually trying to stop me from seeking excellence. Oh, I suppose I could work up a head of steam over the church in her pettiness and cowardice, but I don't feel like it. (The church could snap back with a comprehensive list of my own petty and cowardly actions.) Better, for me anyway, to mind my own business; instead of cursing the darkness, I ask myself why the light is not brighter in my own soul. When did I lower my sights, imagining that it is sufficient to give the mere impression of holiness, that to be simply pious would be enough? Even in our age of low ecclesiology, when we are referred to more often as presiders and celebrants or just plain old Mike than as priests, aren't we still supposed to become the mysteries we touch? Priests aren't the only ones called to great holiness and compassion and sincerity, but we have been called.

†

At the end of vacation or retreat, after having had the leisure to slow down and think about what I am doing and not doing, that's when I often resolve to change my ways. I tell myself that I must do better, that I must not let the grind or inertia or nearsightedness or bad habits get in the way of seeking the spiritual life and following the mission to which I know God is calling me. At such times, I make certain resolutions; I promise myself that I will implement specific plans to reach for the improvement I am hoping to see. Although making such a firm purpose of amendment is the right thing to do, I admit that I have not had much success with it. As soon as I get back in the fray, I am confronted by every practical reason I can't maintain the regimens to which I have committed myself. The patterns are hard to break and the usual chores squeeze me until I give up. And so years pass with too little changing in my life.

The Buddhists have a slogan, "If you can practice even when distracted, you are well trained." That's what I need to find. I want to be like those sheep in the parable about the last judgment at the end of Matthew's gospel. How do I get to the point where I feed the hungry, clothe the naked, visit the imprisoned, and so on, without even noticing that I am doing it? We tell children to "think about what you're doing," but like a skilled athlete or artist, one's inner goodness must become no longer a matter of conscious effort. How can I attain unself-conscious virtue, habits so central to my nature as to be effectively spontaneous? How do I become so well trained in the spiritual life that I will, no matter what, and especially in the midst of the fray, do what's right?

It is not that I don't know what needs to be changed. Like the Psalmist, "I know my offense; my sin is always before me." My faults are obvious, at least the big ones. When I am cruel, I know I should be loving. When I am prejudiced and unfair, I know I am supposed to be open and caring. When I notice that I have been pretty hard on one or another troublesome staff member, I resolve to try to have a better attitude, to be more objective, more understanding and forgiving, something like that. Or if I see that I have been putting on a few pounds and becoming more lethargic, I resolve to work out longer at the gym and to cut out the scotch except on my day off. I see these faults and bad habits as the opposite of the virtues I seek. The Buddhists call these "the far enemies."

The far enemy of love would be hatred, for example. When I strike out against someone, I know it is wrong, of course, but the trouble is that I usually don't see it coming, at least not soon enough to do anything about it. When I run into someone who has hurt me, I have every intention of being forgiving, even of reconciling, just as Jesus asked. But as I start to do this, the person says something I don't like, or maybe doesn't say anything but the intense feelings of betrayal crash back over me anyway. Suddenly, against my firm purpose, I am yelling at him, calling him all sorts of names, criticizing him with judgments that I thought I had given up when I had decided, in my holy recollection, to forgive the bastard.

The Buddhists advise that those who wish to make progress should look a little closer to the virtue they want to practice. Instead of its opposite, they recommend addressing "the near enemies." These are the qualities that look very much like the real virtues, and so can even feel very much like the virtues themselves, but they aren't. By recognizing how they aren't, you can make quicker progress toward what you really want to change. You can get unstuck.

If hatred is the far enemy of love, what might its near enemies be? One is attachment. I see it all the time in parents. A mother loves her son dearly, or so she believes. But there's something uncomfortable about it. Her son feels from her not only her love but a certain expectancy as well, a fearful worry. In my school we have many parents like this; though they love their children, they are also preoccupied with them. If Bobbie gets slugged by Jimmy in the schoolyard, they are ready to bring in the lawyers. If Sandy can't pass the spelling test, they want the sixth-grade teacher to be fired. The near enemy to their love is a clinging attachment, a sense that what happens to the child reflects as much upon the parent as it does on the child.

As priests we have our own problems with this near enemy; we are to love the people of our parish and to tend the flock with generous pastoral care, but we can become just as infected with expectancy and fearful worry as any parent. We get a gnawing charge inside us, and soon we are nagging our people for not being more dedicated to stewardship, or for not being more punctual to Mass, or for not coming to confession, or for lacking the right kind of devotion at Mass or attitude toward the homeless. The near enemy is our own preoccupation with their conversion or lack of it.

We don't love them for their own sakes but for the sake of what their behavior can do to meet some emotional need of our own, or for how it may reflect on "my" parish. It may have been for this kind of anxious worry that Jesus scolded Martha. This near enemy is at my door much more often than the far enemy; I go months without hating anyone but hardly a day without wishing someone would bend to my desires. A neighboring pastor was forced at one point, in self-defense, to announce to his anxious staff, "The parish is not my fault." He refused to give in to the near enemy, the worry that masks itself as pastoral devotion.

In trying to be more compassionate, what might the near enemies be? The one that tempts me often is pity. When I am compassionate, my heart goes out spontaneously and I suffer with the other. I do not keep my distance and my primary goal is not to assign blame, though some discernment about underlying motives may be necessary. The image of compassion is two people sitting side by side, gazing together at the pain or the trouble or the wound. In pity, this is not the case. I am sitting over here and you are sitting over there; I, the helper, am looking at you, the one in need of help. I am feeling sorry for you, you with your problems and the mess you've gotten yourself into. To me, you're a little like a hurt pet, you who are not going to have a very good day today. For this, I am sorry for you but secretly glad for me, since I realize how much better shape I'm in than you. I may have considerable skill in counseling and social work, which I, as the helper, offer to you. And you, who really do need the help, know that I know that you do. This is exactly the distance between us. My pity burdens you with judgment; and it does little to soften my hard heart. It is not compassion but its near enemy.

But another near enemy of compassion is the sense of being completely overwhelmed. When confronted by a real calamity, it is not unusual to feel poor; it can even be a virtue if the Beatitudes are to be believed. But what I feel in calamity, though, is utter powerlessness. When I get called to homes where people have committed suicide, or have to preside at funerals for children or babies who died tragically, nothing I have inside me or possess feels as though it is going to be of any help. Thus, I don't see any purpose in my being involved; all I want to do is keep my distance.

Recently, when a close friend sent me an e-mail informing me that he had been forced to resign from the priesthood for an act of inappropriate touching with an underage teen twenty years ago, I felt that profound helplessness. I felt unable to be there for him but also unable to even touch my own complicated feelings about this terrible turn of events. I did send him a quick note, but then it took me several days to build up the courage to call him. And when I did, I have to admit, it was as much from duty as from a real willingness to enter into his crushing Gehenna.

Remember St. Peter during those wonderful moments when he was walking on the water before the wind and the waves distracted him? To really be compassionate at times when others are in terrible suffering, we must try to focus as he did, albeit momentarily, on the other person instead of our anxiety. Even at times when I am overwhelmed and nearly incapacitated, I find myself often able to ask if there isn't something I *can* do in this situation. *Can I at least call her? Can I at least go over to his house for ten minutes? Can I attend her funeral? Can I pay my respects? Can I phone and ask if there is anything in particular I can do to help?* I am still scared that the waves of helplessness will pull me under, but I keep focused on the suffering other and choose to do at least one thing. Little act by little act, the helplessness dissipates and I find myself doing more than one thing. Over time, my heart finds an opening onto genuine compassion.

Another near enemy of compassion is what may be described as "letting it slide." I confess, it is the near enemy with which I am the most acquainted. Joe, one of my parishioners, feels particularly needy and calls to say he must see Father Mike as soon as possible. I know what will happen: it is going to take an hour and Joe won't take a word of my advice; he will feel sorry for himself for the first half and get angry at God for the second half, and I know that he is using this setting to keep from facing his circumstances. But in the name of compassion, I let it slide. I take the appointment and just sit there with him for the hour, which, as expected, turns into a rerun of the last hour we spent together. This is not real compassion but its near enemy.

Another example. One of the regulars, a poor woman, stops by the parish office—always on weekends because she knows that, unlike the Christian service coordinator, I'm a pushover. In tears, she demands a voucher for a room at the local dive. I know I'm being manipulated, but I tell myself I should just "let it slide" and give her the voucher. Do I really know what it's like to be poor? Besides, it's quicker that way. I do what I do, not out of compassion for her, but for what I want to be able to feel about myself.

†

The large majority of priests are said to be introverts, and so one of our big struggles is the public nature of our ministry. Ray Carey, a priest and therapist, has shown how the requirements of the new liturgy pressure many of us. In the old forms, it was all rubric and blessing; say the right words and do the right things: *ex opere operato*. But now, God save us, we're expected to preside in a personable way, and to do so amiably every time, regardless of how we're feeling. When we are supposed to be present, the far enemy might be detachment, not caring for or engaging with the people, or even with God in prayer. Though we may sometimes feel that way, we hardly find it useful to show our disgust in public. So what do we do instead? One near enemy to being present is sounding holy, another one of our well-known occupational hazards. Most of us have that special voice we can hook up, the one with the polished delivery and practiced cadence. We can sound so holy, especially during Eucharistic Prayer II (which we have memorized), that we imagine that no one notices that we are sleepwalking our way through it. We are a million miles from being present.

But a near enemy can also be trying too hard. Like cheerleaders or exhausted workers in a manic state, we sometimes sound just a little too joyful, impelled by an enthusiasm that seems to have something to prove. Without evident cause, we are suddenly excited, with exclamation points flying in all directions! We call it "passion" but our parishioners are whispering under their breath, "Father, give it a rest."

Those who have served with me know that at certain parish events I expect the priests to do "three times around the room." By that, I mean, yes, you have to go to the reception or dance or fundraiser, but, no, you don't have to camp out for the whole evening unless you want to. You show the support of the priests for whatever this is by working your way around the room sufficiently so that, by the time you leave, most know that you've made an appearance. Well, in trying too hard, I have occasionally taken this technique to embarrassingly ridiculous effects; I enter the room and keep moving, never slowing to listen to anyone or to engage in conversation about any topic of value. I tell folks how beautiful they look. I ask them if they like the food. I point out how well Rose danced that last number. I float, as on a boozy cloud, through the event without ever touching anyone, though I may have hugged scores. That's the near enemy of being present, and I can fight against that almost every weekend.

†

Now we turn to the practice that has been consistently voted best, from generation to generation, century by century, for making progress in the spiritual life. Although I mentioned it earlier, I want to underscore here its importance for us as priests. It is the practice of disclosing one's thoughts to another. No matter how honest you think you are with yourself; no matter how much you think you don't really need to do it (not you, with all your training, your experience, and your education); no matter how convinced you are that this kind of thing is not your "style," as if you are Frank Sinatra and get to have it your way; no matter how embarrassed or self-absorbed you feel when you do it—if you are the least bit serious about holiness or excellence or even just normal human maturity, you need to honestly disclose your thoughts to another or others. If you want to make progress, this is not optional.

Being honest about our sins, fears, tribulations, and weaknesses is painful and leaves us feeling exhausted and vulnerable. Given the chance, this is exactly what we would most like to avoid. But there is no other way. At the very moment we are reduced to painful poverty, Christ often gives us the very things for which we have been longing. "We enter paradise *today*," claims Léon Bloy, "when we are poor and crucified."

Now, by manifesting one's thoughts, I don't mean the usual verbosity that can overtake a gathering of clergy. We all like to share our insights and inspirations and to voice our wisdom and accomplishments. They have their place, but it's not here. The poet Robert Frost used to complain to his students at Amherst that they did not distinguish between thinking and voting. It was clear to him that they began their writing projects already having had the final answer in mind. Their essays usually started with their conclusions, gave three or more reasons why the writer came to these conclusions, and then concluded by repeating these conclusions. "Don't give me a piece in which you tell me how you voted," Frost would demand. "Show me the process of how you think, your meditation." This is how disclosing one's thoughts ought to work.

There's a story told of Abba Poeman being visited by a very charitable anchorite from another land. When they sat down to chat, the anchorite began to speak of the scriptures and of spiritual and heavenly things. When Poeman turned his head aside and said nothing, the anchorite left disappointed. "I have made a long journey in vain," he tells his friend. "For I have come to see the old man and he does not wish to speak to me." The friend goes to Poeman and asks why he refused to speak to the anchorite. Poeman replies, "He is great and speaks of heavenly things and I am lowly and speak of earthly things. If he had spoken of the passions of the soul, I should have replied, but he speaks to me of spiritual things and I know nothing about that." When the anchorite's friend relates what Poeman said, the anchorite is filled with compunction. He then returns to Poeman and begins with the right question, "What should I do, Abba, for the passions of the soul master me?" *Those* are the thoughts that we should disclose to another. If you reveal candidly where you are stuck, where you are fearful, where you are hardened, where you are still unfaithful or uncaring, where you are out of control or close to it, if you disclose that, you are very likely to improve.

"Teach your mouth," Abba Poemen says, "to say that which you have in your heart."

The best way to disclose one's thought is usually through the questions that arise because your life is unhealed.

- *Here's what's happening to me and I wonder what it means.*

- *I want to know if you can help me figure out how I can get past this.*

- *I can't figure out why I am so preoccupied by these thoughts.*

- *Can you tell me if you ever feel such nervousness or insecurity or desolation or loneliness?*

As I said earlier, one could live one's whole life quite happily without the pleasures of sexual intercourse, but to try to live a spiritual life without the intimacy and solidarity of disclosing one's thoughts to another? I doubt it would be anything but miserable, terrifically lonely, and certainly an impossible uphill climb. In our sins and weaknesses and suffering, we can really use that spark of recognition we receive from another, the solidarity of knowing we are not alone. With that, we sometimes find the guts we need to take a big risk or to face the cold shock of an unwelcome truth.

Now with priestly support groups and among our friends, our spiritual directors and at our convocations, we have plenty of opportunities to disclose our thoughts in this way. But we could work a little harder at catching ourselves and one another when we slip off the hard rock of honest disclosure into the swirling stream of opinions and generalizations, the waters where we whip up theological observations and social commentary, where we move, as I mentioned earlier, from the first-person singular to the third-person plural and when we start using the definite article, as in speaking of "*the* priests" and "*the* workaholics" and "*the* staff" and "*the* bishops." There's a place for such discussions, a very important place in rambunctious Catholic life, but it has a lousy track record when it comes to helping us make progress in our spiritual lives. It distances us from our own experience and our personal responsibility.

More candor and transparency, I believe, ought to replace whatever we meant in the past by "clerical culture." If you are willing to do anything "for the honor of the corps," do this. At a recent workshop on sexuality for priests in our diocese, what helped me much more than the lectures was the level of honesty in sharing. We simply need to be brave enough to keep speaking to one another in this way.

Yet, don't forget that none of us is consistently brave. When it comes to disclosure, most of us do well if we bat .300. In a recent article in *America,* an anxious priest is quoted as warning his friend, "Please share on the level at which you think *I* would be comfortable." We have to make allowances for one another, letting each share freely when the time seems opportune to him. If people don't like to have advice shoved down their throats, they hate even more folks who push them up against a wall with their pointed questions. Again, compassion, a willingness to suffer together—this can make us gentle and brave at the same time.

Why is something like personal honesty so important? If you don't disclose your thoughts to another, here's the real danger: you get to keep the secrets you want to keep from yourself. This is perhaps the peril in infantilism that Panikkar worried about, that magical belief, common among kids but still too popular among adults like ourselves, that something doesn't really exist so long as no one mentions it. Earlier I noted how we can simply "not go there" if we are unprepared to face certain realities about our own sexuality. Well, there are lots of places like that, and they are every single place we haven't grown up and don't want to grow up. To be sure the cat doesn't get out of the bag, shut up and make sure others do too.

Never learned how to deal with authority? Well, play it safe and never mention that to others. Over cocktails beef about the bishop or your pastor if you want—in some rectories, this has reached the status of an Olympic event—but don't mention it as a serious topic, as a question you have about yourself.

Got a problem with relating to women? Keep the company of men and don't say a word. Or keep a mile-high wall of courtesy and manners with women so that whatever it is that bugs you will be kept at bay.

Ambitious as the day is long? Don't let the word out, this one especially. Don't let a single soul know how much you would love to be a bishop, or at least a protonotary apostolic. Or don't admit how much you enjoy hearing people use your ecclesiastical title. Or how, if everything is not just so when you celebrate Mass, heads roll in the sacristy afterwards. Or don't let on that you love sitting up front at a meeting with everybody having to listen and cater to you. No, don't mention it. Not if you want to remain in your reassuring near-sightedness. But if you get a momentary burst of daring, then take a chance and tell someone. You might like it; amazingly, candor can grow on you.

Take any of your garden-variety vices. For example, are you envious that so-and-so got all the notice recently and you didn't? Well, why not admit it? Are you mad as hell that the other priest got that lovely parish with no debt and no school and you weren't even asked? What would happen if you actually told someone? Well, they'd know that you're envious, but worse, then you would know it too. And naming it to another makes it so much harder not to do something about it yourself. You might just tip the scales in favor of dealing with it.

Here's a tough one: the other priest in the house or on the other side of town is a lazybones, someone who will work two hours on the phone to get out of a one-hour visit to the nursing home, a fellow who is shameless in asking you to cover for him but who is already booked on the few occasions you ever ask him for a hand. The usual thing is to go ahead and complain about him, to let the whole deanery know how lazy he is. But if you want to make a little progress in the spiritual life, you might have to confess, at least to a close friend, what his behavior really elicits in you. Besides frustration, you might have to admit how jealous you are, how you wish you could get away with what he does but are too proud to pull it off. If you acknowledge that the real reason he bugs you so much is that you're so much like him, only less honest about it, the secret you want to keep from yourself will be out. No way back. You will have to face your darker self as it comes walking toward you.

Thomas Merton said, "The real thing is not eliminating certain pleasures or eliminating certain fulfillments but eliminating illusion." In our humbling disclosures to others, a certain alchemy can take place. As we uncover our unspoken motivations and unacknowledged desires, our illusions are broken down. We come to see ourselves more accurately and know our circumstances in a way that is impossible on our own.

In an odd way, this knowledge of our inner vices and preoccupations is also essential in ministering to our parishioners. Years ago, the great Orthodox metropolitan of London, Archbishop Bloom, gave a series of Lenten talks at Westminster Cathedral. He was a well-known and popular preacher. After one of these lectures, he was standing in the vestibule, accepting praise and words of appreciation from his listeners. A woman came up to him and said, "Archbishop, you must be a very great sinner."

Bloom was surprised but recovered enough to answer graciously, "Yes, Madam, it is true. I am a great sinner." Then he asked, "Do you mind if I ask you how you came to this conclusion?"

"Because you describe our sins so well," she replied.

What we don't or won't see or feel inside ourselves we can't recognize in another. What we avoid in ourselves we will deny to others. If we bury our pain and frustration and failings—as anyone naturally tries to do—we'll lose the little we had, like the gospel's servant who, out of fear, buried his single talent. Each of us has pledged to serve others, but if we set aside enough of ourselves for long enough, those who come to us will recognize nothing in us that can help them. What they are looking for is our poverty.

It is slow moving, this softening of the heart. It opens so little bit by astonishing little bit that you hardly notice the improvement. But its power is cumulative. When you recognize exactly how any courage you ever possessed was nothing less than a grace, this will make it possible for you not to lose patience with those you are trying to support in ministry and in friendship. You'll know exactly how we're all in the same boat, and from that flows an abundance of compassion and heartfelt solidarity. When fear and frailty shimmer in the eyes of a wounded parishioner, you'll be less likely to avert your gaze. Why? Because you will have already seen it in the mirror and heard yourself speak of it to your friend.

[Grace is found in] the bone of the character of a priest who walks to his breakfast with blood on his shoes, the blood of a student who died in his arms in the night after a drunken wreck, the priest is a wreck himself this bright awful dawn, minutes after he blessed the body, but he puts one foot in front of another and walks into a normal day because he is brave enough to keep living, and wise enough to know he has no choice, and he knows he received grace from the hand of the Lord when he needed it most, first when the boy terrified of dying grabbed him by the collar and begged to be told he would live forever and now, here, in the crack of the morning in a campus parking lot as he hesitates by his car, exhausted, rooted.
But he walks.

BRIAN DOYLE

WHAT OLD DOGS LEARN

Of all the orders under God's heaven, we have been the most obliging. In temple times, before Christ's coming, the priests worked as God's butchers and barbecuers. Then, in the early years of the church, the presbyterate gathered around the bishop simply to give advice, all the pastoral dirty work having been left to the deacons and the laity. Later a few of us were sent out from the cathedral to bring the Eucharist to inhabitants of distant farms and homes. Soon the bishop had us preaching and presiding at Eucharist ourselves with those far-flung groups. Then, in what I presume was our only official request, we asked to live at the mission station with the people; the food was better, the people friendly, and it saved wear and tear on the sandals. Thus did we invent the parish, an accomplishment for which we can be justly proud. Of course, to no one's surprise, the farther we got from the bishop, the more we acted like overseers in our own right, which ended up being all right with the bishop so long as we didn't cause too much trouble and sent in the required diocesan assessment. By the Middle Ages, bishops lost interest in our sage advice, and our leadership became less important to our parishioners than what priests did sacramentally in God's name. As long as we took care of the people and did not cause too much scandal, we were free to celebrate the rites for the people and keep the stipends. When we worked as ecclesiastical secretaries in the bishop's chancery, people started calling us "the clergy" because those of our order wore the cassock of the clerical worker. Vatican II restored to us all of these modes of our priestly service, a situation, as I said earlier, that we ought frankly to view as a mixed blessing. But since we are an obliging lot, we adjust; when needed, priests have been able to turn on a dime.

In America's great westward expansion, priests became whatever was needed. Sometimes architects and politicians, often theologians, community organizers, translators, educators, and arbiters of disputes, and very frequently they were and are fund-raisers, builders, and administrators. You name it and a priest has probably been it. Say what you want about the presbyterate, we have been remarkably flexible and generous. Resilience is an old trick of ours, one the church needs now more than ever.

†

While watching television in the days following September 11, I thought of this quality when I came across an interview by Charlie

Rose with the distinguished psychiatrist and writer Robert Jay Lifton. For more than forty years, Lifton had been using his skills to confront some of the most disturbing events of our times— Hiroshima, the Holocaust, the Vietnam War, and the Aum Shinrikyo terrorist cult. He studied how men and women lose and re-create their humanity in these extreme situations. "Survivors can go one of two ways, or usually both ways," Lifton explains; "one is, having touched death, they can close down and remain numbed and really be incapacitated by what they've been through. Or they can confront, in some degree, what they have experienced and derive a certain amount of insight and even wisdom from it that informs their lives." He describes the experience as "a psychic journey to the edge of the world of being."

His voice was a hopeful one in those difficult days. His research shows that we humans are much more resilient than is generally believed; we can mend and grow; we can change and adapt and develop without necessarily losing our sense of ourselves. Even those who have been terrifically traumatized can recover. "One looks into the abyss in order to see beyond it," he explains. In fact, his study shows that the more people nurture that resilience, the more they are able to heal and recover and go on to make differences in the lives of others.

The key is empathy, he says, a sense that one's own sense of self can serve as a model for what it is like to be another human being. Jesus put it a bit more directly: you love your neighbor *as yourself.* It is true that no one *is* me; my life is a unique one. But it is not true that no one is *like* me. How else to love an enemy except by coming to see how that person is *like* oneself? Without that sense of empathy, we tend to see others as threatening, as those who are different, a different generation, a different history, a different color of skin, a different level of education, a different set of theological presuppositions. Sustaining and deepening our sense of empathy are central to pastoral ministry and, in my opinion, given our present circumstances, most endangered among priests.

†

Let's start with one of the things that take up much more of my time than I ever imagined: dealing with complainers. As public persons with leadership responsibilities, we know that people have opinions about us and about what we do, lots of opinions. They also seem to have a growing desire to share these opinions with their priests. This is all to the good when they have been asked to do so on boards, on committees, and at town meetings. But increasingly, people call on the phone or e-mail me or, worst of all, catch me after the early Mass with unsolicited opinions, ones to which they expect me not only to listen but to heed.

Here's an example. The parish secretary says there's someone on the line who wants to speak to the pastor. She's an elderly woman with a thick brogue; let's call her Mrs. O'Brien. Without the least introduction, she tells me she is very concerned about reverence and respect for the Blessed Eucharist at Mass. She informs me that before she called, she prayed to the Holy Spirit for guidance—often, in my book, a troubling sign. She says she is compelled to draw my attention to the very wrong path the parish is taking. I ask her to be a little more specific, and she details two offensive practices that took place at recent Masses. In one, a priest got into what she referred to as "a comedy act" with one of our teens. In the other, "there was—Father, I am not exaggerating here—a skit as part of the homily." I asked her if these two events took place at the Sunday evening Mass, since that is pretty typical of our Youth Mass. She said that, yes, that's when they took place. When I suggest that if they offended her, she might want to consider attending another Mass, she'd have none of it. When I counter that our teens, in my experience, are pretty enthusiastic about their faith, she'd have none of that either. She is a woman not easily cajoled. *Teens should be taught reverence and respect, not catered to. If they want to do those things, they can do them somewhere else, not in front of the Blessed Sacrament.*

We have reached the decisive moment in these kinds of conversation. I know she's not budging and I don't want to budge myself. The only issues on the table therefore are how and how quickly might I bring this conversation to an end. Here are the strategies available to me in such situations:

1. I could tell her to, "Go back to hell where you came from, you old warthog!" The shock it causes is a lot of fun and is often what I actually do feel like saying to complainers, but I have discovered that this approach has almost no chance of ending the conversation in less than five minutes; rather, other conversations are likely, and perhaps letters of complaint sent to the chancery, letters that my bishop is delighted not to receive, thank you very much.

2. I could say, "We just disagree, Mrs. O'Brien." Because Mrs. O'Brien did not call to agree with me but to make sure I agreed with her, there's less than a fifty-fifty chance of ending the conversation quickly.

3. Then there's the "Get over it" strategy. In it, I try to explain to her about liturgical norms or the meaning of Vatican II or the way Life Teen works or any number of theological perspectives on eucharistic devotion. The

drawback here is that because she has no interest in getting over it, it has little chance of ending the conversation in anything approaching the amount of time I want to give it.

4.   Now the final strategy has the great advantage of almost always ending the conversation. What I say is, "Can I put you on hold, Mrs. O'Brien?" and then I come back in a moment and tell her that I have been called to the hospital for an emergency and "we'll have to finish this conversation some other time." This strategy is called "Woops! Gotta go!" It's shameless but it always works.

While I am considering which of these options I shall use, Mrs. O'Brien keeps talking. She is now free-associating about the church. She tells me of the way it was when she grew up in Ireland, a time, she explains, when a parent could have a child baptized if she wanted to, "with no questions asked." This was when "the church didn't give a lot of money away in lawsuits, a time when..." You get the idea. I forget which of the strategies I used, but I got off the phone about twenty minutes later. Then, as soon as I put down the phone, the line occurred to me that I should have used: "And what happened to the days, Mrs. O'Brien, when the likes of you would have had more respect and reverence for the likes of me, a holy priest of God?"

I think we need a more sophisticated approach in our dealings with people who are complaining or demanding or telling us what they think the church or the pastor or the parish ought to do. We tend to identify our initial emotions as what we are really feeling, at least I do, and thereby I react out of my rawest and least obliging emotions. My emotional wiring is entirely too primitive for the task at hand; it's like using an old circuit breaker when what is needed is the latest Pentium chip.

Some of us are too easily wounded and we brood over episodes of confrontation. That's me. (After all, I can still recall almost every detail of my conversation with Mrs. O'Brien.) People like me keep going over the fight in our minds. We imagine what would have been a better answer, or a reply that might have more easily satisfied the other person, or the perfect response to such a complaint, regardless of whether the listener agrees with it or not. Or we speculate as to why we had to be the one singled out to be the object of this complaining abuse. Other priests have thicker skins; they don't take the confrontation so personally. It's all part of the job. They converse with the complainer in a voice that almost sounds like someone else's, the quiet voice of reason, which gets softer and calmer as the other gets louder and more agitated. And some of us have a mixture of both these traits.

Years ago I attended a leadership workshop with a couple of my friends. We thought we had signed up for a week of pleasant conferences; we were looking forward to lovely evenings out to dinner in the Bay Area. We had obviously not read the brochure closely enough. Halfway through the opening session, one of my friends leaned over to me and whispered under his breath, "This is going to be The Workshop from Hell," and he was right. The emphasis was on *work*. We trained, we practiced, we often failed miserably, but slowly a few lights went on and we started to get into a different swing of things. We endured this hell week for the same reason football players do: to get in better shape and to learn new techniques. Despite ourselves, these old dogs were learning new tricks.

The central skill I developed was how to keep listening, even in a difficult encounter; I practiced engaging another until I could do it more honestly and with greater personal freedom. I learned how to remain engaged without allowing myself to be pushed to places I did not want to go, either by the other or by my own habitual reactions. I discovered how to gauge my own reactions. *What am I actually feeling and why am I feeling it? Does she remind me of my mother, whom I never quite figured out how to confront? Or am I just overly tired this evening? She might have a good point, this Mrs. O'Brien, though I wish she didn't have to be so shrill about it. What do I want to do here? Is this something important enough to me to engage all my emotions?*

A person with thicker skin might have to learn how to keep from immediately writing off Mrs. O'Brien as one of those "nuts" who don't understand, or won't grow up, or has an ax to grind against the church. (In the clergy abuse conflagration, you hear plenty of our voices filled with this kind of disavowal: *"There they go again, blaming celibacy or the bishops or the victims."*) He might learn to keep listening carefully to Mrs. O'Brien to find out why she feels so strongly. Why is this issue so important to her? He might discover her "real" issue; the reverence concern might be masking a deeper wound. Why, for example, did she bring up that issue of baptizing a baby "with no questions asked"? There may be a lot behind her demanding words, things she may not yet have recognized in herself. If such a person kept listening to her and asking her questions instead of lecturing her or only trying to get her to tow the party line on this reverence topic, something might happen. Many times it won't, but it surely won't if we don't learn to have greater emotional flexibility and generosity in our dealings with those who disagree with us.

On the other hand, people in pain sometimes desperately want you to take responsibility for how *they* feel. They think of it as a job to which everyone in the church has agreed. *Father, what are you going to do about this?* I have come across, however, no command-ment requiring us to be the midwives of others' emotions. We can understand how someone feels, we can see if there is something appropriate the church can do to alleviate the painful aspects of those feelings, but the feelings remain and must remain the other's.

The only feelings for which we can be responsible are our own. And our hearts serve best when they are not always open or always closed but when each of us has a door in which he lets in what he thinks deserves to get in and bars the door to those things that are unfair, untrue, or cruel. Our explanations and beliefs should come into play but not as ways to distance ourselves from or to con-trol the Mrs. O'Briens in our parishes. No one should talk us out of our principles, but there's no reason we can't also express our own emotions, especially our compassion. Even self-righteous, time-consuming complainers are hurting human beings; there is a reason they have become so brittle. When we attend to the pain, we are sometimes able to help.

With emotional maturity, we can also be tough-minded in our communication. By "tough-minded" I mean that the goal is real communication, not spin or getting it over with. This is where my strategies, all four of them, have to be tossed out the window or at least monitored closely so they aren't used to manipulate. In real communication I take others and their concerns seriously, but I also insist that I be taken seriously myself along with my own concerns. Amma Sarah's thought is helpful here: "If I prayed to God that all men should approve my conduct, I should find myself a penitent at the door of each one, but I shall rather pray that my heart may be pure towards all."

A simple example: A few years ago, after I removed some very tired, burnt-orange shag carpeting from the sanctuary, one of my parishioners came up, all huffy and furrowed, "You need to know, Father, that some people are leaving this parish because you took the carpet out of the sanctuary." I looked at her with sincere astonishment, too shocked to say anything but the truth: "I can well understand why people would be upset with what I am doing around here. I am making a lot of changes, and I can easily understand why some might want to go to another parish. But, I gotta tell you, that filthy orange carpet is not a reason to leave this parish. I'm sorry. It just isn't." Then, to her credit, my parishioner caught herself and laughed.

Real communication is morally committed. It has a goal. There's something I want out of all the effort to communicate with others, especially the pained and the complaining. I want to discover a communality; I want to see and feel what binds us together. In the long run, I don't want to make Mrs. O'Brien happy; I want to be her companion in the body of the church.

I gave a pastor's night on the clergy abuse scandal recently, and one of the people who sidled up to me afterwards was a woman whose son had been molested years ago by a priest. She shared with me her suffering, how guilty she felt that she had not noticed more, had not done something back then, how her son never went on to high school, how he is always in trouble with the law and messed up with drugs and never seems to be able to keep a job. She even told me that he suffered from attention deficit disorder. I wondered where all this was going, and then it occurred to me, it was not going anywhere. She heard the pain in my voice when I talked about what has happened to children in our church and how we needed to make amends. She felt she had found a companion to her long-suffering. She called me on the phone a week later to tell me she had done some research about support groups for victims and she wanted to give the information to me; she knew her son would never go to such a group, but she felt that I might be able to direct someone else to help.

†

The priest today is a man on the clock, a guy with one foot out the door, even when he is doing inspiring priestly work. He hears the constant "tick-tock, tick-tock." Our ministry today is of necessity often a high-volume operation, a fate we share with the likes of St. Paul and St. Francis Xavier. But because of this, I notice in me an undesirable lowering of the level of my engagement. I come in with the paramedics; I anoint dear Bill; I pray with his family; and then I pass him and his family on to the pastoral-care team. All this is practical and necessary. But when real empathy is missing, people notice, even if they don't complain about it to me. It is the essential pastoral act through which divine grace finds a home. I am in the process of training myself to be there, utterly there, in whatever pastoral circumstance requires me. Empathy does not require a particular number of minutes, only my generous and focused attention. Then my priestly presence can become a window revealing God's shepherding love.

At those times when I am called to the shocked chaos of the emergency room, I feel as I often do at prayer. I find it very hard to stay in the tension of that moment; everything inside me is looking for the exits. I have no shortage of reasonable excuses for leaving as quickly as possible: *The family deserves their privacy. The nurses have asked us to keep our visits short. I'm really an outsider here. Besides, I've anointed her; there's nothing left to do.* But the truth is that I hate being so close to that suffering that threatens to open into an abyss.

May I tell you how I cope? It's not pretty but it works. Most of the time, I start off angry. *The damn family waits until the middle of the night, of course, even though Miss Mary has been critical for the last three days.* Or I may be irritated because I'm not on duty but Father On-Duty can't be found, and so off I go resentfully. Or I may be frustrated because I was having a pleasant day and the last thing I wanted to do was confront sickness and sorrow. Or I may be disappointed because these next few minutes may well be enough to push right off the edge of the table everything else I had hoped to accomplish today. If someone were to see me driving toward the hospital, they would eye a red-faced, screaming fool in a clerical collar. But I have discovered that if I get it out, it can then be over with. I can scream like the old lady scolding the unjust judge, if it will help. And most of the time, it does work. With sufficient time and a little grace, I arrive at the hospital no longer wanting to get it over with as quickly as possible. By the time I get to the doors of the emergency room, enough of it is out of my system that I am ready to meet whatever surprise or out-of-control situation I find. I can linger. I can wait. I can let it all take as long as it needs to take, this moment with these people whom, as a priest, I have been given a chance to love. If suffering is what they are doing, I can join them. Yes, it is *their* suffering—I may never have met Miss Mary until this moment—but I can be their companion. I don't have to try like crazy to do something about their pain or to turn it into something else, even comforting faith. I befriend them. If faith is theirs in that moment, they will find it themselves or receive it as a grace as we pray and listen to one another.

With the incarnation, Jesus took our flesh; he took all our circumstances, every single one of them but sin, and he even made himself "to be sin who did not know sin, so that in him we might become the righteousness of God" (2 Cor 5:21). If I wish to act *in persona Christi*, I must do the same and strive to embrace what I see and not rush past what strikes me as strange or troubling or repulsive or depressing in the lives of those given to my care. If I see people as problems, that's what they'll be. Without knowing their poverty as my own, I will offer no more than an illusion of compassion, something that will touch no one and change nothing. An aloof priest can't do his job; he can only *look* as if he's doing his job.

†

The church is going through what everybody on earth is going through. The real overarching issue of our times is that the way of life we have lived for centuries is ending; societies across the globe are all in various states of fragmentation. One of the largest migrations in the history of the planet is taking place; already 120 million people live in countries where they were not born, many of them making their homes in our own country, including not a few of the priests who serve in our dioceses. We are most certainly *metido en la masa,* caught in the mix. Few of us live in the same world that we were "given" at birth.

Since we are only at the beginning of this age, whatever it may turn out to be can't be seen yet, at least not to me. So far the experience has been almost entirely one of dislocation. That is why what is going on in our church is less about pre– and post–Vatican II ideologies than about the experience of being disoriented. (This may explain why our *Catholic Update* series has not been the remedy that we thought it might.)

It may get expressed in ways theological and psychological, but it is primarily a cultural phenomenon. When I replay Mrs. O'Brien's complaints in my head and add other similar phone calls, e-mails, and conversations to it, I notice that these folks are almost always talking about their roots, about their early experiences as a

Catholic or, with the younger ones, their sense that they missed out on something essential. They all want the church to go back to the "good old days," though each describes or imagines a different set of good old days. I sense they are nostalgic for predictability, for the time when what they expected matched what they got.

T. S. Eliot defined culture as simple as "that which makes life worth living." It is what we take for granted, what makes us laugh or cry, the given before we know there's a given. It is what informs our spontaneous responses. Culture specifies value. Love this. Flee from that. Love reverence and respect. Beware of spontaneity and revealing one's feelings in public. Do you express your devotion by quiet prayer before the Blessed Sacrament or by witnessing to where your faith intersects with daily life? What's the value for you? (I do not tell this to Mrs. O'Brien, but I am more in her cultural camp than she thinks. I like the quiet and measured myself. When everyone claps during the recessional at the Spanish Mass, I clap too; but there is a difference: they are into it and I feel a little silly.) We Catholics get into fights because each of us wants to believe that there is just one Catholic culture, by which we mean our own native one, of course. *By the standards of my Catholic culture, the church nowadays has got it wrong. The value must be this, not that, just the way it was when I was growing up or when I came into the church.* Like their burgers, Catholics want their religion "their way."

†

In this context, think of what we put the poor mother of Jesus through. On the solemnity of the Immaculate Conception, I lead her tall porcelain figure, encircled by flashing electric stars and fat cherubs of clay, into the parish hall and begin the Nicaraguan festivities with the jubilant question *"¿Quién causa tanta alegría?"* A few days later I am up before dawn celebrating Mass with the pregnant *mestizo* image of Guadalupe at my side. In May, our Filipinos begin our *Festa ni Maria* with a lengthy procession in which everyone—very well dressed and ordered according to rank in their elaborate and imponderable pecking order—places a flower at Our Lady's feet. When I finally reach the sanctuary, I crown the flower-bedecked, dark-skinned statue from Antipolo with the help of one of several women dressed in long, white gowns.

Always serene and welcoming in her wildly different garb, Mary possesses all the characteristics of the peoples who make up our parishes; her skin is every human color. She incarnates the diverse qualities we love. It is not surprising that Mary remains so popular in this time of global disequilibrium; she offers the considerable comfort of a mother's breast to those who feel adrift outside the predictability of native culture and land.

Admittedly, as far back as the council of Jerusalem, we have made the distinction between transcendent faith and its cultural expression. One faith, many rituals. One mystery, many theologies. The Gentiles can eat their bacon if they want, just so long as they contribute to the collection for the poor. But have we pushed this diversity too far, getting away from the very Catholic notion of, well, catholicity? Each group gets a Madonna in their own image and likeness, right down to the footwear and the trim on the halo. *This is our virgin, and no one else's.*

To each, she is a mother, and in complicated ways, she is known under all these guises as the mother of Jesus, but to all of us together, who is she? How do we see her? Is she merely a projection of our diverse yearnings? How does this virgin, this Madonna, this young girl have anything in common with the woman revealed in the gospel and described in theological tradition? Will the *real* Virgin Mary please stand up?

The argument is sometimes made that the immigrants who are devoted to these images are simple people and they, naturally, express their faith in simple ways. I find this both patronizing and untrue of my parishioners. People said things like this, generations ago, of my Irish ancestors, who turned out, by and large, to be sufficiently able to endure education, complexity, and the irony that brings an end to innocence but the beginning of wisdom. The faith is not so blind that only the naïve can believe it. Rather, it was the failure of preachers, teachers, and pastors, folks like ourselves, to provide adequate companionship for those who made the journey toward greater complexity. When they no longer wished to live as exiles, whom did they meet on the new road? Not us, at least not often enough. This may be one reason so many came to abandon a too simple faith as they became more sophisticated. It is argued that their prosperity made them worldly and secular; I think that came, when it did, after loneliness.

Much is said dismissively nowadays of "consumer Catholics." We look down our noses at them because, unlike our enlightened selves, they are caught up in the virus of *affluenza,* the desire for more and more goods, services, and personal attention, even from the church. Use the term if you like, but remember, in part we made them that way. One of the great unintended consequences of reorienting our parishes toward service is that we taught them to believe that somebody was always "at your service." When we asked the people to identify their needs and express their desires, we implicitly agreed to try to meet them, sometimes all of them. In this mistaken name of service, we have striven valiantly to become "all things to all people" by giving each what he or she wants. No offense, but it is now past time, I believe, to admit that it hasn't worked out as we had hoped. In our generosity, and our need to be liked, we have unwittingly formed a whole generation of Catholics to be passive receivers of sacramental and spiritual realities. We need to be welcoming and willing to adjust to people's circumstances, yes, but our parishioners belong not only to a church that they can call upon but one that calls upon them to live out vocations of selfless love and service.

To stereotype our demanding parishioners or to shun those of different cultures are ways we distance ourselves from the very people we've promised to serve. Remember how we did that a generation ago with those who "didn't get it" after Vatican II? You see how well that served us! They did not go away and they did not become silent; what they became was angry and even more demanding and, in some cases, very well organized. If we want to, I think we can find ways to see beyond reactions—our own and theirs—to communal responses that might bring us closer together.

Don't imagine that it will be simple or painless. Living together is never easy, even within the same culture and background; just think of life in any family. And so you have to expect that there's going to be plenty of disorientation and difficulty in living as Christian communities, especially ones that are as diverse and in as much transition as ours certainly are.

It's a dicey operation at best, this aim of friendship, even unity, in the Spirit. The church has ever been "a company of strangers." Except for Jesus, do you think tax collectors would ever have mingled with fishermen? St. Paul had to confront the Corinthians for their cliques and their conflicts. The council of Jerusalem was needed because those of different cultures could not agree on what Jesus expected of his followers. So we need to be less surprised by the pressures, to learn to expect them as normal. I think we can do as we do in physical exercise: we can train ourselves; we can build up the pastoral muscles needed to address them. In time, we may come to see how the pain in these trials is something we can learn from, something that purifies and presses us forward in simple, healthy, human ways. George Steiner once said, "No one has ever learned or achieved anything worth having without being stretched beyond themselves, till their bones crack. 'Easy does it,' says America to mankind. But easy has never done it. Never."

†

My barber is a wonderful young mother. She told me that she was at the park with her two-year-old son the other day. He had been sitting on the slide and another two-year-old came over. Wanting to sit in the same place, he shoved her son off. She saw this but didn't think it was anything worth worrying about. In short order, though, the father of the other two-year-old came over to apologize, very embarrassed, which she thought was hilarious. "My son knows these things happen in the play yard," she replied to the father, "and if he doesn't, it's about time for him to learn."

"At issue…is the capacity to absorb suffering and learn from it," says Lifton. That's how survivors survive. What we usually do with pain is put up with it; we take up the cross, offer it up, endure the turmoil. We turn the other cheek, at least we're supposed to; sometimes, in our own pain, we don't. But even when we are able to turn the other cheek, even when we endure suffering, our jaw remains clenched. We need to start thinking about what our disorienting pain can become. How to give our jaws a rest, that's what we need to figure out.

Timothy Radcliffe once asked his Dominican confrere Chrys McVey, who has served in Pakistan for forty years, how long he would remain, given all the problems, persecutions, and dashed hopes. He replied, "Until I am tired of dying." Paul spoke similarly to the Romans, saying, "For your sake we are being killed all the day; we are looked upon as sheep to be slaughtered." And so we are. We are suffering. Yes, the priesthood is a difficult life right now, but it is a life, and it's ours, and I think we can gain something from it even under pressure and suspicion. Our lives can grow. They can expand if we are willing to put out the effort. Our sufferings can transform us if, in them, we can find the "grinding of the heart," which "touches it deeply."

We must guard against that "grinding that is disorderly and harmful, which only leads to defeat." We can become numb or defensive, as if finding escape or relief were our primary goals. St. Paul admitted that he felt he was being "poured out like a libation" (Phil 2:17; 2 Tim 4:6). But he told the Corinthians, "We do not lose heart. Even though our outer nature is wasting away, our inner nature is being renewed day by day" (2 Cor 4:16). As Paul Dudziak points out, "He was poured out, but not burnt out."

We get the spiritual life and the parishes and the presbyterates we really want, the ones we plead for in prayer and are willing to work toward, the ones we invest ourselves in, put our shoulders to, and willingly take risks to reach. "Although tenderness has its place," the novelist Mark Helprin has written, "life is driven not by tenderness but by vigor."

†

Our world is now *the* world, the whole world, a circumstance that should fit our catholicity nicely, but it's been pretty rocky so far. We have done well enough finding our faith in our various cultures, but what of the faith beyond culture? In these days, one of a priest's crucial tasks may be to witness to the mystery as something found in but essentially beyond anything of our own making and, in particular, to bring the bigger world of faith to bear on whatever tends to keep people divided and suspicious. In the early days of the Bible, Chrys McVey reminds us, "it is written that 'Anyone who wished to consult the Lord would go to the meeting tent outside the camp' (Exod 33:7). 'Outside the camp' is where we meet God. Outside the institution, outside culturally conditioned beliefs and perceptions, 'outside the camp,' God speaks to us 'face to face' (Exod 33:11). It is outside the camp that we meet a God who cannot be controlled. And it is outside the camp that we meet the Other who is different—and discover who we are. And where our home really is." One traditional way of attending to this transcendence was the ancient practice of facing our churches toward the east, the region of the dawn. It reminded the congregants to look beyond their individual lives, to remember that we are all, in the end, sojourners destined for a kingdom beyond the horizon.

More than others, priests, bishops, and, to a lesser degree, deacons belong outside the camp. We are not to be partisans, neither agents of any culture nor leaders of any narrowly defined group. Neither should we seek to be in charge of the camp, no matter how much we love our culture, our subgroup, or our society. Leave that to others. Cardinal Suenens underscored this task in a famous speech during the Second Vatican Council in which, quoting Pope Pius X, he said: "The church does not evangelize by civilizing, but civilizes by evangelizing." That is why priests must be the foreigners at the center of the community, the ones who will not allow faith to be tied too closely to one human way of seeing or acting. Whatever remains mystifying about God's ways, we certainly do know that they are not domestic. We turn our faces toward the dawn to witness that the things of God do not belong to us but to God. "Seek God," advises Abba Sisoes, "and not where he dwells."

†

Under the pressures of ministry today, we have sometimes resized our ministry to fit our own "comfort zone." If we can swing it, we make sure we don't have to take orders from anyone or have to deal with the messy situations. Although an understandable reaction, it is another indication of spiritual immaturity. We're supposed to be the ones who can work with others, not just tell them what to do; we've been ordained to be men with backbone, the ones ready to face trouble, not run from it. St. Ambrose stipulated that a priest should have both faith and mature character. "It is not enough to have only one of these qualities; he must have both, together with good deeds to prove it."

If anything is clear so far in this new era for the priesthood in America, it is that people simply are not going to put up with our immaturity. Go ahead if you want, try and get your parishioners to do what suits you. Keep asking the secretary to cover for you. Demand that your staff carry out your unpopular policies. Make a big scene; insist on your prerogatives as a priest. But let me warn you: in my opinion, you are going to be less and less successful. People are tired of it. And they don't buy it; even the pious ones don't. They will write you off. Because he won't go where they need him to go, a priest who will only serve where he feels at ease is not worth their effort.

Our interactive way of determining pastoral assignments nowadays has many virtues, but one great danger remains: what happens if the priests we still have only take those parishes with no debt, no school, and no divisions? With everyone grasping for the "plums," who will go to the places at the bottom of the barrel? Who, in short, is ready, like Christ, to live and die with the suffering and the poor? Without generous priests (and the deacons, religious, and laity to collaborate with them), without all sorts of folks willing to give themselves to difficult assignments and ready to do so with enormous enthusiasm and creativity, without those motivated by a love that yearns to do the grueling and to overcome the daunting, there will be no martyrs, no witnesses to the extraordinary presence of Christ.

†

I return again to St. Peter, dear old reckless Peter. The boat is his, but we meet him still out on the water, the place, he assures us, where we too belong. Yes, he is knocked about by enormous waves and the winds rage around him; he knows the times are desperate. But from these he is distracted momentarily by the reassuring face of Jesus. He knows his own frailty, for he will be quick to accept the rescuing hand of his Savior, glad to have hold of it.

To the extent we are unwilling to join him there, unwilling to take the attendant risk that we could, like him, end up flailing about, looking silly and nearly drowning, we will look as cowardly and sound as whiny as we are. *Please, please, please, come to the seminary,* we plead. But what do we teach them to do in the seminaries? To be as bright and creative as they can? To take chances? To be ready for a life of sacrifice? Do we train them for resilience and generosity? Do we insist they manifest a capacity to live intimately and maturely upon this planet? And why should we expect it of them if we don't expect it of ourselves? This is my prediction: until we change our ways, the young will not see the excitement in our way of life. The dreamers, the talented ones, the visionaries and geniuses, the ones

God may indeed be calling, they'll go somewhere else with their enormous energy. Instead we will continue to attract men in early middle age, those, excuse me for saying this, ready to settle down.

"Please, please, please get involved in our parishes," we implore our parishioners. But what do we ask of them? To give out communion? To donate sacrificially? To attend one of our self-help seminars or Bible studies? To jump through the hoops of our sacramental preparation? Where is the excitement in that? Where is the call to real service, for trusting faith in troubling times? We have come to consider high attendance at anything as a sign of success; we have forgotten that, on Pentecost, the standard was a bit higher: people had to be on fire.

After the Edict of Milan, the vitality of the local churches went into decline for a variety of social and religious reasons, not the least of which was the popularity and upwardly mobile benefits of being a baptized Christian. Not everywhere but often, there developed an inverse proportion: the more people were baptized, the more diluted did the zeal of the community become. In many places, the church became so tame that if you had a strong spiritual impulse, you had no place to go but to run out to the desert or shut yourself up in a cloister. Later you had to become a mendicant or a missionary if you wanted to give expression to your call. One of Vatican II's dreams was to renew parishes with holiness strong and plentiful enough to sustain the life of the Spirit in our neighborhoods and within our cities. The hope was to build parishes filled with saints and martyrs, to live our lives among folks with enough faith to revive among us this lost art of walking on water.

We have heard Peter's story so many times, we jump to the ending. We remember as a reproach Jesus' words to Peter after he saved him from drowning, "O man of little faith, why did you doubt?" But wait. Go back. Look. See those stunning moments when Peter stood there on his own. One like us actually *did walk on water*. Isn't that remarkable? And if such has been done once, the argument goes, it certainly can be done again. Could it be that turbulent waters are in fact the best suited for walking? With our eyes on Christ, I believe the whole church can find the faith we need. And when, as is likely, we do tumble in, we'll find his saving hand grasping ours as Peter did. I prefer to understand Jesus' question kiddingly: *Why were you so worried, Peter, with me as your lifeguard?*

To follow Peter's example demands we take a very big risk as priests and human beings. We'd all prefer to be known for our skills, our talents, our attractions, our accomplishments, our shining brilliance. But our parishioners need us to be poor before them, to be ourselves, and to explore the life of faith in front of them and with them. Television has the Naked Chef, a man with a reputation for exuberance and not taking himself too seriously. At this moment, the church may need priests who are metaphorically naked, a community of transparent ministers ready to be honest in communication and willing to let ourselves be seen as the apostles let themselves be seen, well, up until Luke buffed them up for his Acts of the Apostles. As has often been the case in the history of the church, the baptized trust more those leaders courageous enough not to hide their fears and mistakes, those who let themselves be seen drowning and worse. I think our parishioners want fewer of our bright ideas and more of our empathy and honest response to life. In short, they are attracted to priests who know how to take chances—not just any chance and not simply for the sake of the thrill—but chances they perceive are prompted by the Holy Spirit;

from such priests parishioners will find the guts to be courageous and docile disciples themselves.

†

Merciful God, grant us unwearied hearts, hearts that seek less to be satisfied than to be set on fire, less to be secure than to take the risks your Spirit inspires. Let that Spirit move among us, with guidance and renewal, so that we may see beyond the dusty but comforting surfaces. As you did long ago, make each of us "like one come out of an upper room," to borrow from the Irish poet, Seamus Heaney, "To fret no more and walk abroad confirmed."

SELECT BIBLIOGRAPHY

The following works are either quoted in the text or helped inform and deepen its content.

Albacete, Lorenzo   "The Struggle with Celibacy." *New York Times Magazine,* 28 April 2002.

Brown, Peter   *Authority and the Sacred: Aspects of the Christianisation of the Roman World.* Cambridge University Press, 1997.
The Body and Society: Men, Women, and Sexual Renunciation in Early Christianity. Cambridge University Press, 1988.

Brown, Raymond, S.S.   *The Community of the Beloved Disciple.* Paulist Press, 1979.

Chödrön, Pema   *The Places That Scare You: A Guide to Fearlessness in Difficult Times.* Shambhala, 2001.
When Things Fall Apart: Heart Advice for Difficult Times. Shambhala, 2000.

Doyle, Brian   *Credo.* St. Mary's Press, 1999.

Evdokimov, Paul   *Ages of the Spiritual Life.* St. Vladimir's Seminary Press, 1998.

Goergen, Donald, O.P.   *The Sexual Celibate.* Harper San Francisco, 1975.

Heaney, Seamus   *Electric Light.* Farrar, Straus and Giroux, 2001.

Lifton, Robert Jay   *The Protean Self: Human Resilience in an Age of Fragmentation.* Basic Books, 1994.

"Evil, the Self, and Survival: Conversation with Robert Jay Lifton," interview with Harry Kreisler in *Conversations in History,* produced at Institute of International Studies, University of California, Berkeley, 1999.

McVey, Chrys, O.P.   "Outside the Camp." *Priests & People,* January 2002.

Moody, Rick   *The Black Veil: A Memoir with Digressions.* Little, Brown, 2002.

Moore, Sebastian   *Jesus the Liberator of Desire.* Crossroad, 1989.

O'Connor, Flannery   *The Habit of Being: Letters of Flannery O'Connor.* Edited by Sally Fitzgerald. Farrar, Straus and Giroux, 1988.

Papesh, Michael L.   "Farewell to 'the Club,' on the Demise of Clerical Culture." *America,* May 13, 2002.

Paz, Octavio   *The Double Flame: Love and Eroticism.* Harcourt, 1996.

Radcliffe, Timothy   *I Call You Friends.* Continuum, 2001.
Sing a New Song: The Christian Vocation. Templegate, 1999.

Rich, Adrienne   "Women and Honor: Some Notes on Lying." In *The Best American Essays of the Century.* Edited by Joyce Carol Oates and Robert Atwan. Houghton Mifflin, 2001.

Robinson, Marilynne   *The Death of Adam: Essays on Modern Thought.* Houghton Mifflin, 1998.

Rodriguez, Richard   *Brown: The Last Discovery of America.* Viking Penguin, 2002.

Solomon, Andrew   *The Noonday Demon: An Atlas of Depression.* Scribner, 2001.

Sullivan, Andrew

Love Undetectable: Notes on Friendship, Sex, and Survival. Vintage Books, 1998.

Ward, Benedicta, trans.

The Sayings of the Desert Fathers. Cistercian Publications, 1972.